THE SIGN OF THE 3&3 FACTOR

WILLIAM R. PRIEBE

Published by The Consolidated Christian Commemoration

Caledon Township, Ontario, Canada

The Cover Explained

* The Biblical sign of Jonah is portrayed on the book cover here with 2 equilateral triangles that pivot on the same central axis point on the same plane as attributed to the AD 34 Sabbatical year. Each triangle represents a total time duration of about 72 hours in length.

The dark colored triangle (in the foreground) within the Hebrew month of Nisan represents the regulatory "3 days & 3 nights" (Mth 12:39, 40) time period in the grave as required between our Lord Yehoshua's (Jesus') actual Wednesday crucifixion with His resurrection day ensuing on the weekly Saturday Sabbath.

The light colored triangle (in the background) within the Hebrew month of Sivan represents the regulatory "not many days hence" (Acts 1:5) time period between our Lord's day of ascension on a Wednesday with the founding New Covenant Church's actual debut day of Pentecost proceeding on the weekly Saturday Sabbath.

These overlapping triangles are placed 43 days apart from the Lord's Day shown in the month of Nisan pointing closely to the top position in a clockwise formation on a 360 degree circular plane representing a Hebrew 354 (29.5 x 12) days + a 30 day intercalary month (Adar II) = a 384 day agricultural based Sabbatical calendar year.

Our Lord's crucifixion 'cut off' was accomplished exactly on the 69th Sabbatical (Shemitah) year of AD 34 in the Hebrew 3794 year fulfilling the conditional terms of Daniel's Chapter 9 Old Testament prophecy.

.

The Sign of Jonah is similar in appearance to the Star of Solomon where the combined points of each triangle represent one day of creation completing furthermore with the seventh day as the Lord's Day, a Sabbath day, the rest day of God's perfection.

* * * * * * * * * * * * * * * * * * * *

If these are the last days then all hidden treasures of God's Word shall surface. Every rock will be over turned and every truth shall be revealed for the harvesting of knowledge to those who might take notice.

Through the centuries people have interpreted God's Word in accordance to the times in which they have lived. Yet many have remained oblivious to the actual logic intended by the Bible authors of earlier times whom gave testimony under God's inspiration. So it is that the sign of Jonah is a hiatuses (a gap of time) with little sought meaning. Yet ever so prevalent was the sign reiterated throughout the Word by our Lord Yehoshua (Jesus) Himself regarding the specified terms for the fulfillment of His own bodily resurrection. Thus being a paradox for some and a total mystery to others.

Therefore in summary of the Bible as a whole, to what merit with any major significance should the sign of Jonah realistically have or hold? Was the sign merely a figurative statement on an isolated parable? Can a more literal sense be gathered from it? Could it be put more into a formal conclusion? What other historical documents make reference to such? Does it relate directly to our Lord's Day as we break collectively to understand it? If so, do we truly recognize God's risen day as initially declared through the Greek scriptures?

What if we as a Church have been caught up into a dogmatic rule of ordinances and have missed the key essential point for some time along? When presumably revealed, would we shift our position to take notice of the timing in question? Would we give rise to our Lord's countenance?

Thus the Lord Yehoshua (Jesus) declared "that no sign would be given but the sign of Jonah" as revealed to a tumultuous generation. Perhaps to be discerned as a great apostasy unraveling the very core within the Church itself through this discourse of which I am forthcoming to contend.

- William R. Priebe

Dedicated in loving memory of the late Pmary65

TABLE of CONTENTS

.

(Since the time this works was completed some web addresses may have been subject to change)

Part A The Preponderance of Evidence:

Sec. 1 Biblical & Non-Biblical

* Here we shall see that Jews recognise Sabbaths every 7th day on a weekly basis, count a 7 week period of weekly Sabbaths between Passover to Pentecost, observe 7 High (great) Day annual Sabbaths, and every repetitive 7th year is a Sabbatical year considered sacred on the Hebrew Calendar. The realization of these various types of Sabbaths overall is the essential key in identifying the correct time table behind God's prophetic schedule.

However, the post timing traditionally observed behind the event of Yehoshua's (Jesus') Passion is based purportedly on a Nicene presupposition with a mis-interpretive translation of the Gospel's resurrection passages. There a narrow minded theory had been reasoned and adapted to mainstream Christiandom for a timing of Yehoshua's Passion with Him being crucified late on the day of a Good Friday (preparation day) and resurrecting early on the day of an Easter Sunday (the first day of the week) morning.

This wide-stream belief stemmed primarily due to the revised Church-state ruling mandated at the Council of Nicaea in AD 325 by Emperor 'Constantine the Great' as a non-vocal but very persuasive influential bystander through Eusebius of Caesarea with the other attending Bishops to transition a fixed annual 'Easter Sunday' apart from God's preferenced 7th day Sabbath. Thus being an inline move reinforcing the model pattern of resting every weekly Sun-day from AD 321 on forward as a way of constitution granted to the Gentile Christian Church for worshipping along side all other existing pagan religions of the fourth century Roman Empire.

Thus a new man-made premise in the past did incur for the Church away from the divine Will of God when the Council members whom met waived their timely recommendations to comply with the Emperor's command of reasoning Bible scripture merely to suit his own religious agenda while suppressing the true chronological meaning behind the Gospel resurrection passages.

Furthermore the Sabbath practice of resting on the seventh day was officially abrogated in the intermediate Church's Canon laws at the Council of Laodicea in AD 363. There the new Church paradigm was established based on the former misconception (contrary to keeping God's Sabbath commandment) as set forward to be adopted by most Christian Masses in general being misconstrued inconspicuously on up through the ages up into our present modern day.

Hence-forth, the 'Sunday' worship policy took off rapidly infusing 'the first day of the week' phrase into scripture without our Lord's Day being recognized on "one of the Sabbaths" (mia ton sabbaton) as uniformly described in all of the original Gospel accounts of the earlier Greek Bible New Testament Texts.

 Thus being an accurate literary detail conveyed furthermore in other literal Bible translations of God's Word but often less recognised though showing the ever-consistent 'mia ton sabbaton' details of the Passion event in Yehoshua's time.

* The true Lord's Day occurring literally on a Sabbath day was in essence; mis-understood, misinterpreted, mistranslated, reallocated, reconstituted, and substituted by the Emperor's mainstream overall fundamental position of settling on weekly Sun-day (the first day of the

week) worship acting contrarily to all of which the original Word of God actually teaches.

* Whereas;

Jonah 1:17

"Now the LORD had prepared a great fish to swallow up Jonah. And Jonah was in the belly of the fish, three days and three nights."

Daniel 7:25

"And he (Constantine the Great) shall speak great words against the most High, and shall wear out the saints of the most High, and think to change times and laws: and they shall be given into his hand until a time and times and the dividing of time."

Daniel 9:25, 26

"Know therefore and understand, that from the going forth of the commandment to restore and to build Jerusalem unto the Messiah the Prince shall be seven weeks, and threescore and two weeks: the street shall be built again, and the wall, even in troublous times. And after threescore and two weeks shall the Messiah (Yehoshaua) be cut off"...

Hence the Messiah the Prince was 'cut off' and crucified in a year when the set scriptural proponents must have applied:

Matthew 12:8

"For the Son of man is Lord even of the sabbath day."

Matthew 12:39, 40

"But He answered and said unto them, An evil and adulterous generation seeketh after a sign; and there shall no sign be given to it, but the sign of the prophet Jonah: For as Jonah was three days and three nights in the whale's belly; so shall the Son of man be three days and three nights in the heart of the earth."

Matthew 16:4 "A wicked and adulterous generation seeketh after a sign; and there shall no sign be given unto it, but the sign of the prophet Jonah. And he left them, and departed."

Matthew 27:63 "Saying, Sir, we remember that the deceiver said, while He was yet alive, after three days I will rise again."

Mark 2:27, 28 "And He said unto them, the sabbath was made for man, and not man for the sabbath. Therefore the Son of man is Lord also of the sabbath."

Mark 8:31 "And He began to teach them, that the Son of man must suffer many things, and be rejected of the elders, and of the chief priests, and scribes, and be killed, and after three days rise again."

Luke 6:5 "And He said unto them, that the Son of man is Lord also of the sabbath."

Luke 11:29 "And when the people were gathered thick together, he began to say, This is an evil generation: they seek a sign; and there shall no sign be given it, but the sign of Jonah the prophet."

John 11:9 "Jesus (Yehoshua) answered, Are there not twelve hours (of light) in the day?"...

Acts 1:5 (on the day of ascension)

"For John truly baptized with water; but ye shall be baptized with the Holy Ghost (on the day of Pentecost) in not many days hence."

* Note – All unmarked Scriptural quotes are taken from the Authorised 1611 King James Version along with every instance of the KJV transliterated word 'Jonas' being corrected to 'Jonah' as it appears within the original Greek.

* Note – Parentheses is supplemented in round (brackets).

* Therefore;

In careful hindsight an essential all in depth chronological re-evaluation of the Passion event should clarify the true meaning behind the 'Sign of Jonah' as prophetically fulfilled through God's eternal salvation plan. I hereby offer a critical review regarding the crucifixion and resurrection events.

Here we shall re-assess the pertinent points of interest in an investigation to obtain a realistic comprehensive understanding of the actual Lord's Day.

Hopefully an enlightenment may be remedied to those whom possess the earnest desire for a truth of clarity in; 'The Sign of Jonah'.

** The true essence of understanding Jewish chronology is modeled from the recorded beginning of creation with the reckoning of Hebrew time as stated in Genesis 1:4,5; "And God saw the light, that it was good: and God divided the light from the darkness. And God called the light Day, and the darkness he called Night. And the evening and the morning were the first day."

The other verses in Genesis 1:8, 13, 19, 23, and 31 say; "And the evening and the morning were the (e.g. second, third, fourth...etc.) day". Thus complying that each and every day (e.g. 24 hr. period) began and ended consecutively from 'sunset to sunset' as between 2 evenings .

The Jewish authors of the Old Testament and the New Testament understood inclusively that the next Day period always began with night darkness and was followed by daylight in the morning. The night time hours were divided into 4 equal interval watches (i.e. Mth 14:25) and the daylight time were divided into 12 equal hours. Thus the day cycle was always deemed and observed from 'sunset to sunset'.

The New Testament backs this up in John 11:9 when Yehoshua states; "Are there not 12 hours (of light) in the day? If any man walk in the day he stumbleth not, because he seeth the light of this world."

In regards to the timing of Passover the Jewish Historian Josephus (AD~70) clarifies; (Quote Begins)

"So the high priests, upon the coming of their feast which is called the Passover, when they slay their sacrifices, from the ninth hour till the eleventh, but so that a company not less then ten belong to every sacrifice, and many of us are twenty in a company."

(Quote Ends) Wars of the Jews 6:9:3 William Whiston – 1998 Thomas Nelson Publishers.

Here in a modern reckoning of a time from about 2:00 p.m. to 5:00 p.m. The Passover lamb would then be prepared for roasting over an open fire on the Hebrew Spring time month of Nisan 14th in the last few remaining hours of the day ending in the twelfth hour around 6:00 p.m.. The Pascal Seder Supper would then follow after sunset on the nightly beginning of Nisan 15th. Here reads, Exodus 12:8; "And they shall eat the flesh in that night, roast with fire, and unleavened bread; and with bitter herbs they shall eat it."

What you need to recognize is the word 'Passover' to a Jew in Yehoshua's time was a loose – common term that was applied generally to a whole celebration period of about eight days. Nisan 14 was the Passover eve reserved for the ritual of ceremonial preparedness. Nisan 15-21 was the feast of unleavened bread which lasted for seven days where Jews adhered to the strict rules of cleanliness. On Nisan 15 commencing at night was a large Seder banquet with roasted lamb and unleavened bread followed by fasting where Jews ate only unleavened bread for the remaining six days from Nisan 16-21 as a harsh reminder of their vast exodus (i.e. Deut 16:8). The whole feast of unleavened bread was re-enacted with a diet of flat wafers depicting the former event when yeast could not rise for a total time of seven days as Jews fled passing over Egypt while led out by God as their protector.

Leviticus 23:5 "In the fourteenth day of the first month at even (when the moon is determined as a full moon) is the LORD'S passover."

Numbers 9:5 "And they kept the passover on the fourteenth day of the first month at even (when the late afternoon sun is setting down) in the wilderness of Sinai: according to all that the LORD commanded Moses, so did the children of Israel."

Luke 22:1 "Now the feast of unleavened bread (Nisan 15-21) drew nigh, which is (also) called the Passover."

Here the Jewish Historian Josephus (AD~70) says; (All Quotes Begin)

"So the Hebrews went out of Egypt, while the Egyptians wept...it is that in memory...we keep a *feast* for eight days."

(Quote Ends) The Antiquities of the Jews, Book 2 Chapter 15 Line 315-7 William Whiston – 1998 Thomas Nelson Publishers

*Note - here the word *feast* is in italics and is very misconstrued which has been supplanted by the Translator. A more appropriate word here in the terms described could have read simply as 'a vigil'.

The Jewish Pharisee Historian Josephus (AD~70) continues to clarify with particular references to the Passover period in several places as follows; (All Quotes Begin)

"In the month of Xanthicus which is by us called Nisan...on the fourteenth day of the lunar month...every year slay the sacrifice...which was called the Passover..." and Josephus continues; "The feast of unleavened bread succeeds that of the Passover and falls on the fifteenth day of the month, and continues seven days, wherein they feed on unleavened bread..." (Antiquities of the Jews 3:10:5) William Whiston

Antiquities of the Jews 3:10:5 – 1998 Thomas Nelson Publishers

Josephus attested elsewhere; "As this happened at the time when the feast of unleavened bread (Nisan 15-21) was celebrated, which we call the Passover..." (Antiquities of the Jews 14:2:1) and "As the Jews were celebrating the feast of unleavened bread (Nisan 15-21), which we call the Passover it was common for the priests..." Antiquities of the Jews 18:2:2 William Whiston – 1998 Thomas Nelson Publishers

Consider as well; "They left Egypt in the month Xanthicus, on the fifteenth day of the lunar month; four hundred and thirty years after our fore-father Abraham came into Canann..."

(All Quotes End) Antiquities of the Jews 2:15:2 William Whiston – 1998 Thomas Nelson Publishers

Furthermore...

"Remember the commandment which the Lord commanded thee concerning the Passover, that thou shouldst celebrate it in it's season on the fourteenth of the first month, that thou shouldst kill it before its evening, and that they should eat it by night on the evening of the fifteenth from the time of the setting of the sun." (Quote Ends)

The Book of Jubilees 49:1 (160~BC) Translated by Robert H. Charles 1914

http://www.summascriptura.com/html/Jubilees_RHC.html

As well...

"And they departed from Rameses in the first month, on the fifteenth day of the first month; on the morrow of the Passover the children of Israel went out with a high hand in the sight of all the Egyptians." Numbers 33:3

The Apostle Paul's wonderful statement; "Purge out therefore the old leaven, that ye may be a new lump, as ye are unleavened. For Christ our Passover is sacrificed for us: Therefore let us keep the feast, not with old leaven (Nisan 14), neither with the leaven of malice and wickedness; but with the unleavened bread (Nisan 15-21) of sincerity and truth."

1 Corinthians 5:7,8

These events were willfully organized and re-enacted as partaken by Yehoshua with His disciples when they fulfilled the Passover Seder ceremony on Nisan 15 being the 'πρωτη ημερα των αζυμων' as the 'first day of unleavened (bread)' being described from Matthew 26:17,20,21 ; Mark 14:12,17,18 ; Luke 22:7,14 giving reference to the former night that commemorated the Israelite forefathers' beginning of departure to freedom from slavery in Egypt.

* Greek Biblical exegesis is often cited with the Interpreter's misconceived theological beliefs. On the difficult passages, exegesis should be formulated through sensible theological debate. In the traditional belief for a Friday Nisan 14 crucifixion day in AD 30 or AD 33 the big picture suggests interesting details;

- There Yehoshua and his disciples could not have traveled on the weekly Sabbath of Saturday Nisan 8th arriving in Bethany six days (Jhn

12:1) before the Passover beginning on Friday Nisan 14th. Sabbath travel was imperatively limited (e.g. Joshua 3:3,4) in accordance to Hebrew law.

- Also our Lord with His disciples are erroneously denied (cut short) to have kept the ceremonial traditional Passover Seder which was customarily observed in the night at the beginning of Nisan 15th on 'the first day of unleavened bread' as Scripture reveals (i.e. Ex 12:8; Mth 26:17; Mrk 14:12; Luk 22:7).

- Clearly on the beginning of Nisan 15th the roasted lamb was consecrated by the Jews through oral ingestion when our Lord with the disciples partook of their Seder banquet together with the required timing of the Passover meal.

- The Passover fellowship setting as described in St. John 13:1 was an anticipatory meal gathering immediately prior to the actual feast. Many Scholars however interpret this (early Friday Nisan 14th) setting to have been Yehoshua's final meal perceived at a pre-mature time when the Sanhedrin's uncustomary night-time judicial hearing was thought to have followed afterwards. There along with Annas, Caiaphas, Herod Antipas, 3 reproaches by Pilate (Luk 23:22), and before the vast throngs of peoples on a couple occasions, these busy events could not have occurred within a narrow time line of about 16 hours or less, for a mock sentencing, judgment, and crucifixion (Mrk 15:25) of Yehoshua.

* The same gesture is similarly in line with a Wednesday crucifixion belief as well. This view is commonly shared by many believing that Yehoshua was buried in AD 31 on the late afternoon of Wednesday Nisan 14th as the Passover preparation day (Jhn 19:31) to Thursday Nisan 15th (Holy Convocation Day) fulfilling the conditional Sign of Jonah (Mth 12:39, 40) being '3 days & 3 nights in the heart of the earth',

and Mth 27:63 & Mrk 8:31 'after 3 days'. There in a context with a resurrection moment occurring on the late afternoon of Saturday Nisan 17th with a chronological arrangement of its own;

- Hence the temple cleansing and upsetting of money changers (Mrk 11:15) coincided on the weekly Saturday Sabbath of Nisan 10 (i.e. the day of procurement - Ex 12:3) four days prior to the Passover on Wednesday Nisan 14. However, the handling of livestock (i.e. Ex 20:10), buying and purchasing, were totally prohibited on Sabbath days in stringent abidance to Jewish custom and law.

** In order to have the Gospel's Passion chronology put into a reasonable perspective, a more feasible time line regarding the crucifixion and resurrection events was essential. Let us consider a median near the 'middle-end' of our Lord's final Passover period.

To acquire such a median let us reconsider a linguistic approach from the ORIGINAL Koine Greek Texts for the resurrection passages at; Matthew 28:1; Mark 16:2; Luke 24:1; and St. John 20:1,19 of the New Testament.

In these verses we commonly find the Koine Greek phrase; 'μιαν σαββατων' or 'μια των σαββατων' which is transliterated as 'mia ton sabbaton' and is directly translated to literally mean on; 'one of the sabbaths'. As well, similar words can be found within other New Testament verses such as; Acts 20:7 : 1 Corinthians 16:2 and partially in Colossians 2:16.

This phrase has been traditionally perceived, interpreted, and understood to read as 'the first day of the week', or less commonly as 'the first of sabbaths'. However, let us consider specifically the Koine Greek word 'σαββατων' which is transliterated as 'sabbaton' where the literal English rendering is translated as 'sabbaths' and is plural of meaning in line with Greek Syntax rules.

In the key resurrection verse of Matthew 28:1 (below) the original Koine Greek word 'σαββατων' appears twice in the same sentence and is plural in meaning at both instances;

"οψε δε σαββατων τη επιφωσκουση εις μιαν σαββατων ηλθεν μαρια η μαγδαληνη και η αλλη μαρια θεωρησαι τον ταφον"

GREEK TEXT – STEPHENS (Editor) 1550 – TEXTUS RECEPTUS

The full sentence of Matthew 28:1 would render closely like;

"Late (οψε) but (δε) sabbaths (σαββατων) to the (τη) lighting-up (επιφωσκουση) into (εις) one of (μιαν) sabbaths (σαββατων) Mary (μαρια) Magdalene (μαγδαληνη) and (και) the (η) other (αλλη) Mary (μαρια) observed (θεωρησαι) the (τον) sepulchre (ταφον)."

What could this possibly mean according to Greek Syntax with the contrasting 'sabbaths' in the very same sentence having a duality sense of definition with a co-existence between one and another??

Hence, Matthew 28:1 is describing details in meaning like; 'Late (adverb) (post-after-end) (genitive of separation) but (with exception of the annual Passover) sabbaths (plural) as it was lighting up (twi-lighting e.g. Psm 148:3) on one (a cardinal number) of the (a partitive- genitive case function) sabbaths (plural)...... (etc).

 Thus a description that pertains to a time interval when the Passover festal period was finished and had already completed (e.g. 'End', opse-adverbial) the 2 High sabbaths (Nisan 15 & 21 i.e. Ex 12:16) of the Passover period onto a weekly sabbath (1 of 7) or one sabbath (Nisan 23) from a group of seven weekly sabbaths within the 50 day counted duration of time between Passover (i.e. from the sheaf offering - Lev 23:11,15,16) leading up to Pentecost.

Then, Yehoshua would have arrived at Bethany on Friday Nisan 8th being six days (Jhn 12:1) before the Passover (preparation day) on Thursday Nisan 14th (full moon), and ate the Passover meal (on the first day of unleavevened bread) at the precise designated time (Mth 26:17, Mrk 14:12, Luke 22:7) on the nightly beginning of Friday Nisan 15th. He was cut off in AD 34 being the prophetic 69th Sabbatical year (Dan 9:25,26) since the temple of Jerusalem had been reconstructed on Nisan in 445 BC.

There He was crucified on Wednesday Nisan 20th on the Passover preparation day (Jhn 19:31) before Thursday Nisan 21 = the seventh day of unleavened bread (a Holy Convocation Day) and would resurrect '3 days and 3 nights' later (Sign of Jonah/Mth 12:39, 40) on the weekly Sabbath late afternoon of Saturday Nisan 23rd. This particular Divine inspired day being one integral Sabbath in a week of (7) sabbaths within the 50 day period leading up to Pentecost.

Thus Leviticus 23:15 would read and apply to this time setting;

"And ye shall count unto you from the morrow (Saturday Nisan 16th) after the (High) sabbath (Friday Nisan 15th), from (after) the day that ye brought the sheaf of the wave offering (Saturday Nisan 16th); seven (weekly) sabbaths shall be complete:"

This group or week of weekly Sabbaths for the Hebrew 3794th year (since recorded creation) in AD 34 should have been Nisan 23rd, Nisan

30th, Iyyar 7th, Iyyar 14th, Iyyar 21rst, Iyyar 28th, and Sivan 6th. Here Yehoshua resurrected on the first weekly Sabbath of a group of 7 weekly Sabbaths therefore being on 'one of sabbaths'. Thus 'Pentecost' arrived later on Saturday Sivan 6th being on the 'seventh day' of consecutive weekly sabbaths (after the sheaf offering day passed on Nisan 16) as the 50th day, and three full days after the day of ascension on Wednesday Sivan the 3rd being 40 days from the resurrection day.

* Here along with the resurrection event, the 50 day omer count commenced after the High (Annual) Passover Sabbath (Friday) of Nisan 15th where both the sheaf offering (Saturday Nisan 16th), and the day of Pentecost (Saturday Sivan 6th) coincided simultaneously on weekly Sabbaths for that particular Sabbatical (69th) year of AD 34 as a specification to Yehoshua (Jesus) being Lord of all Sabbaths.

Leviticus 23:16 reads;

"Even unto the (counted) morrow after (or on) the seventh sabbath (as a hep-tad group of seven weekly sabbaths) shall ye number fifty days; and ye shall offer a new meal offering unto the Lord."

*Note – By construing properly from the correct source point of reference, the 50 day omer counting does NOT necessarily commence year after year from the first day of the week (after the weekly sabbath in the Passover period), where Pentecost is calculated by the Gentiles to repeat collectively on a continual Sunday basis.

Leviticus 23:11 reads;

"And he shall wave the sheaf before the Lord, to be accepted for you: on the next day (Nisan 16th) after the (high) sabbath (Nisan 15th) the priest shall wave it."

A clear account by Historian Flavius Josephus (AD~70) describes when the omer count (i.e. Lev 23:11) commenced in his book 'The Antiquities of the Jews' book 3 chapter 10 paragraph 5 line 250 follows;

(Quote Begins)

"But on the second day of unleavened bread, which is the sixteenth day of the month (Nisan), they partake of the fruits of the earth, for before that day they do not touch them."

(Quote Ends) William Whiston -1998 Thomas Nelson Publishers

* Philo Judaeus (20 BC – AD 50) a Hellenistic Jewish philosopher is stated; (Quote Begins)

" There is also a festival on the (Nisan 16) day of the pascal feast, which succeeds the first day (Nisan 15), and this is named the sheaf, from what takes place on it, for the sheaf is brought to the alter as a first fruit…"

 (Quote Ends) 'THE WORKS OF PHILO JUDAEUS' by C.D. YONGE, Vol. III LONDON 1855

The Greek Septuagint (LXX) Old Testament (~270 BC) clarifies when the Passover sheaf offering was offered in Leviticus 23: 11 ; (Quote Begins)

"…and he (the priest) shall lift up the sheaf before the Lord, to be accepted for you. On the morrow (Nisan 16) of the first day (Nisan 15) the priest shall lift it up."

 (Quote Ends) Sir Charles Lee Brenton Lancelot. Published by Samuel Bagster & Sons, Ltd. London 1851 See the Online Septuagint at;

http://ecmarsh.com/lxx/Leviticus/index.htm

*Note – The custom of dedicating the ripened 'first fruits' barley offering (Ex 15:19-21) to God Almighty was observed on whatever weekday the 16th of Nisan fell upon for each particular year. Thus being the observation by Jews from the earliest days right on up through the middle ages into modern times.

To support this chronological arrangement overall, the widely overlooked verse of St. Luke 6:1 underlies a principal that Jews were in recognition of a series of Sabbaths between Passover and Pentecost thus reading;

"And it came to pass on the second sabbath after the first, that he went through the cornfields and his disciples plucked the ears of corn and did eat rubbing them in their hands." KJV

This verse has created much debate amongst bible commentators as to what the 'second Sabbath after the first' could mean. In 'Adam Clarke's Bible Commentary' we receive an analysis from him and some other various Commentators giving their explanations for the meaning behind the Luke 6:1 passage;

(Quotes Begin)

"The Vulgar Latin renders δευτεροπρωτον, secundoprimum, which is literal and right. We translate it, the second Sabbath after the first, which is directly wrong; for it should have been the first Sabbath after the second day of the passover. On the 14th of Nisan, the passover lamb was killed; the next day (the 15th) was the first day of the feast of unleavened bread; the day following (the 16th), the wave sheaf was offered, pursuant to the law, on the morrow after the Sabbath: Leviticus 23:11. The Sabbath, here, is not the seventh day of the week, but the first day of the feast of unleavened bread, let it fall on what day of the week it would. That and the seventh day of that feast were holy convocations, and therefore are here called Sabbaths. The morrow, therefore, after the Sabbath, i.e. the 16th day of Nisan, was the day in which the wave sheaf was offered; and after that seven Sabbaths were counted, and fifty days completed, and the fiftieth day inclusively was the day of pentecost."

"ενσαββατω δευτεροπρωτω, In the first Sabbath after the second." What does this mean? In answering this question, commentators are greatly divided. Dr. Whitby speaks thus: "After the first day of the passover, (which was a Sabbath, Exodus 12:16,) ye shall count unto you seven Sabbaths complete, Leviticus 23:15, reckoning that day for the first of the first week, which was therefore called, δευτεροπρωτον, the first Sabbath from (after) the second day of unleavened bread; (the 16th of the month;) the second was called, δευτεροδευτερον, the second Sabbath from that day; and the third, δευτεροτριτον, the third Sabbath from the second day; and so on, till they came to the seventh Sabbath from that day, i.e. to the 49th day, which was the day of Pentecost."

"The mention of the seven Sabbaths, to be numbered with relation to this second day, answers all that Grotius objects against this exposition." WHITBY'S Notes.

"I think, with many commentators, that this transaction happened on the first Sabbath of the month Nisan; that is, after the second day of the feast of unleavened bread. We may well suppose that our Lord and his disciples were on their way from Jerusalem to Galilee, after having kept the passover. Bp. NEWCOME."

"Now these Sabbaths, between the passover and pentecost, were called the first, second, Sabbaths after the second day of the feast of unleavened bread. This Sabbath, then, on which the disciples plucked the ears of corn, was the first Sabbath after that second day. Dr. Lightfoot has demonstrably proved this to be the meaning of this 'σαββατονδευτεροπρωτον' (Hor. Hebraic. in locum,) and from him F. Lamy and Dr. Whitby have so explained it."

"This Sabbath could not fall before the passover, because, till the second day of that feast, no Jew might eat either bread or parched corn, or green ears, Leviticus 23:14.) Had the disciples then gathered these ears of corn on any Sabbath before the passover, they would have broken two laws instead of one: and for the breach of these two laws they would infallibly have been accused; whereas now they broke only one, (plucking the ears of standing corn with one's hand, being expressly allowed in the law, (Deuteronomy 23:25,) which was that of the Sabbath. They took a liberty which the law gave them upon any other day; and our Lord vindicated them in what they did now, in the manner we see. Nor can this fact be laid after pentecost; because then the harvest was fully in. Within that interval, therefore, this Sabbath happened; and this is a plain determination of the time, according to the Jewish ways of reckoning, founded upon the text of Moses's law itself."

Dr. WOTTON'S Miscellaneous Discourses,

"The word δευτεροπρωτω, the second first, is omitted by BL, four others, Syriac, later Arabic, all the Persic, Coptic, AEthiopic, and three of the Itala. A note in the margin of the later Syriac says, this is not in all copies.

"The above MSS. read the verse thus: It came to pass, that he walked through the corn fields on a Sabbath day. I suppose they omitted the above word, because they found it difficult to fix the meaning, which has been too much the case in other instances."

(All Quotes End) 'The New Testament of Our Lord and Savior Jesus Christ with a Commentary and Critical Notes' by Adam Clarke – published by Peter D. Meyers, New York, 1835

* The series of weekly Sabbaths between the Passover Sheaf Offering and Pentecost signified a moment in fulfillment of God's promise for the freedom and liberty to all descendents with lineage of the ancestral fore-fathers on route to the Promised land. These Sabbaths may have been referred to by the Jews in the Old Testament time as the 'Queen of Sabbaths' which were embraced as a bride in affection of Yehovah's direct guidance and total fullness forth-coming. The significance is mirrored in the New Testament which underlies in the transliterated phrase 'mia ton sabbaton' (one of the sabbaths) with 'mia' in the Greek feminine gender. There the feminized 'one of sabbaths' is expressed quite uniformly throughout all of the N.T. resurrection passages and may represent a solemn day of soulful matrimony like a queen bequeathed to her bride-groom being our true Lord Yehoshua himself. Thus all believers from every ethical background are delivered from the bondage of sin and death through Yehoshua's resurrected victory (achieved on that special Sabbath day) being newly preserved through the Holy Spirit onto eternal life as everlasting.

The verse of Mark 16:9 in the original Greek reads 'πρώτη σάββατου' transliterated as 'protos sabbatou' which is translated literally to mean either the 'first / primary / chief (ordinal) sabbath (singular)'. Here in the long ending of Mark 16:9 – 20 regarded as an extension that does not exist in the earlier and older manuscripts. The author (interpolater) there may have been referring either to the creation Sabbath as it was preeminent in nature for the seventh day cycle of weekly rest, or the resurrection day occurring on the first weekly sabbath after the Sheaf Offering Day on Nisan 6th. Therefore, the 'past sabbath' mentioned in Mark 16:1 would have chronologically been Thursday Nisan 21st the high sabbath which completed the Passover period.

*Note – The phrase the 'first day of the week' could have appeared originally as; 'πρώτο ημέρα του εβδομάδας' and transliterated as 'prote hemera tis hebdomata' in the original Greek texts for the verses of; Matthew 28:1, Mark 16:2, Luke 24:1, St. John 20:1,19; Acts 20:7, and 1 Corinthians 16:2 in the New Testament but does not appear anywhere in any way, shape or form.

The word 'εβδομάδας' in the Koine Greek for 'week' does appear in certain contexts of the Greek Septuagint LXX Old Testament (~270BC) in; Ex 34:22; Lev 23:15, 16, 25; Num 28:26; Deut 16:9, 10, 16: II Chron 8:13, and Dan 9:24, 25, 26, 27; 10:2, 3 respectively.

Also Luke 18:12 reads; "I fast twice in the week, I give tithes of all that I possess."

* Note that this passage has bemused many Bible Commentators. The word "week" here is not derived from 'εβδομάδας' in the Koine Greek Text transliterated as 'hebdomata' but changed from the source word "σαββατου" transliterated as "sabbatou" meaning 'sabbath' in English and being singular in meaning. The author here in Luke 18:12 is describing that they fast on 2 separate weekly sabbath. Thus the use of the word "week" here is inappropriate and oddly idiomatic and should have been conveyed normally as the "sabbath" to define it more correctly.

The first century Greek writing of the 'Didache' in 8:1 reveals that the Judeans fasted on the second and fifth sabbaths (σαββατων = sabbaton) that were fittingly recognized within part order to the week of seven weekly sabbaths being observed between Passover and Pentecost.

(i.e. Lev 23:15)

Please see The Didache 8:1 Greek – English Interlinear at;

http://home.earthlink.net/~dybel/Documents/Didachellnr.htm

Any day before a high-great (annual) sabbath (Holy Convocation) day or a weekly sabbath within the Passover period was regarded as a preparation day. Thus Yehoshua died on a Passover preparation day before the last day of the Passover feast shown as a great 'μεγάλη' sabbath as stated in John 19:31 (YLT). Compare also to John 7:37 describing 'μεγάλη' as a 'great' occasion being the 'last day' in the feast of Tabernacles. The great/high/annual sabbath stated in St. John 19:31 (after the preparation day) was the 7th final (Holy Convocation) day of the Passover feast and occurred on a Thursday Nisan 21st in the 3794 year of AD 34. The final (7th) day of unleavened bread in the Passover feast that commemorated the Israelite fore-father's deliverance from bondage in Egypt.

Consider; The Didascalia Apostolorum (AD~230) Oxford: Clarendon Press 1929

R. Hugh Connolly – Translator, CHAPTER XXI (Quote Begins)

"I ate My Pascha with you, and in the night they apprehended Me...because thereon they crucified Me, in the midst of their festival of unleavened bread." (Quotes End)

Consider; The Apostolic Constitutions of the Holy Fathers (AD~375) – Book V Chapter XVII & XVIII

(Quotes Begin)

"Keep your nights of watching in the middle of the days of unleavened bread. And when the Jews are feasting, do you fast and wail over them, because on the day of their feast they crucified Christ; and while they are lamenting and eating unleavened bread in bitterness, do you feast." con't...

"Do you therefore fast on the days of the Passover, beginning from the second day (Nisan 16th) of the week (feast-period) until the preparation (Nisan 20th), and the Sabbath (Nisan 21st), six days (Nisan 16, 17, 18, 19, 20, 21), making use of only bread, and salt, and herbs, and water for your drink."

(Quotes End)

The text used here is translated from 'Greek' by William Whiston and was revised and reprinted by Irah Chase, D.D. (D. Appleton & CO. New York 1840)

* Note – The 'preparation day' described above on Nisan 20th is adequate in comparison to the 'preparation day' of the crucifixion as described in Mrk 15:42, Luk 23:54, and St. Jhn 19:14.

Exodus 12:16 "And in the first day (Nisan 15) there shall be an holy convocation, and in the seventh day (Nisan 21) there shall be an holy convocation to you; no manner of work shall be done in them, save that which every man must eat, that only may be done of you."

Leviticus 23:4 "These are the feasts of the LORD, even holy convocations, which ye shall proclaim in their seasons."

Leviticus 23:5 "In the fourteenth day of the first month at even is the LORD'S passover."

Leviticus 23:6 "And on the fifteenth day of the same month is the feast of unleavened bread unto the LORD: seven days ye must eat unleavened bread."

Leviticus 23:7 "In the first day ye (Nisan 15) shall have an holy convocation: ye shall do no servile work therein."

Leviticus 23:8 "But ye shall offer an offering made by fire unto the LORD seven days: in the seventh day (Nisan 21) is a holy convocation: ye shall do no servile work therein."

Numbers 28:18 "In the first day (Nisan 15) shall be an holy convocation; ye shall do no manner of servile work therein:"

Numbers 28:25 "And on the seventh day (Nisan 21) ye shall have an holy convocation; ye shall do no servile work."

Consider a non-Canonical reference; The Apocryphal Gospel of St. Peter (AD~190) in verse 12 being a moment in time after the crucifixion following the completion of the Passover 7 days period when the disciples were clearly in bereavement and the resurrection event had not yet been fulfilled. (Quotes Begin)

"Now it was the last day of unleavened bread (Nisan 21), and many went out of the city (Nisan 22) returning to their houses, the feast (Nisan 15-21) being at an end. And we the twelve disciples of the Lord wept and were in sorrow, and every man withdrew to his house sorrowing for that which had come to pass."

(Quotes End) H.B. Swete – Translator, MacMillan and Co.

In this Passion narrative the next day outside of the completed Passover period was a secular day allowing for the buying and preparation of spices for the burial of Yehoshua's body. Thus Mark 16:1 states;

"And when the (high) sabbath (Thursday Nisan 21st) was past, Mary Magdalene, and Mary the mother of James, and Salome, had bought sweet spices, that they might come and anoint him." Then in Luke 23:56 it says; "And they returned, and prepared spices and ointments; and (later) rested the (weekly) sabbath day (Saturday Nisan 23rd) according to the commandment."

Here the Gospel biblical evidence indicates that the preparation of spices and ointments by the woman occurred on the secular day of

Friday Nisan 22nd between the two contrasting Sabbaths held on separate days. Their intent was likely to anoint Yehoshua's body immediately after the weekend sabbath had finished.

Likewise, the 'Gospel of Nicodemus' a chapter from 'Gesta Pilati' the Roman Passion account (AD~350 ?) reveals that the body of Yehoshua would have decayed for about a day and a half before a customary burial by Joseph.

The rash burial consisted initially with a purchased 'one piece garment cloth' placed around Yehoshua's body on the late Wednesday evening. After the Thursday 'high' sabbath passed (i.e. Jhn 19:31), Joseph returns to the tomb (likely with Pilate's permission) on Friday Nisan 22 (secular day) with fine 'linen strips' and an ornate headdress, and wraps the body with aromatic spices (under a guarded watch) completing the customary task well before the weekly Sabbath begins.

The linen strips and headdress are re-discovered (Jhn 20:5) neatly rolled up on the late evening of Saturday (mia ton sabbaton) Nisan 23 being the weekly sabbath when Peter comes to the sepulcher. The guards quickly bring word to the priests who seek for Joseph (who was placed earlier into a secured holding cell under house arrest) knowing that he was the last person working in the tomb (i.e. The Gospel of Nicodemus) but he was missing, and not revealed until 40 days later.

This narrative does not suit a Friday to Sunday Passion chronology too well.

The sign of Jonah also leaves little merit when the missing Joseph was with the raised Yehoshua at the tomb on the late evening time of the weekly sabbath after a traditionally believed Good Friday crucifixion. (i.e. Luk 24:4)

"And it came to pass, as they were much perplexed thereabout, behold, two men stood by them in shining garments."

* The Hebrew sacred calendar year was comprised of 7 annual (high days) Sabbaths (See Lev Ch.23). These were the Feasts of; Passover on the first month of Nisan 15th, 21st: Pentecost on the third month of Sivan 6th : Trumpets on the seventh month of Tishri 1st : the Day of Atonement on the seventh month of Tishri 10th : Tabernacles on the seventh month of Tishri 15th and the 22nd. The appointment of these 'High Sabbaths' (Holy Convocation Days) were regulated and officiated by the Sanhedrin Council who formerly observed lunar cycles prior to the fall of Jerusalem in AD~69.

When the Jewish race later became dispersed (diaspora) living globally in different time zones, all major religious holidays were extended by an extra day from Hillel II (AD~367) establishing intercalary principles that enabled observers everywhere to celebrate in unison on a worldwide basis.

The months of the Hebrew calendar were; Nisan, Iyyar, Sivan, Tammuz, Ab, Elul, Tishri, Marchesvan, Chislev, Tebeth, Shebat, Adar, and Adar II as an intercalary (leap) month. The month of Tishri was on the first month of the civil calendar and was the seventh month on the Jewish religious calendar. The month of Nisan was the seventh month on the civil calendar and was the first month of the Jewish religious calendar.

* Yehoshua affirmed His position of authority;

"For the Son of man is Lord even of the sabbath day." St. Matthew 12:8

"And He said unto them, The sabbath was made for man, and not man for the sabbath. Therefore the Son of man is Lord also of the sabbath." St. Mark 2:27, 28

"And He said unto them, That the Son of man is Lord also of the sabbath." St. Luke 6:5

* Note – No where in the New Testament does it say He was 'Lord of the first day of the week' being the supposed day of His resurrection.

* A Warning for a Future Tribulation;

"But pray that your flight be not in the winter, neither on the sabbath day." St. Matthew 24:20

The New Testament evidence confirms that the Passover lamb was replaced wholly by Yehoshua's body and blood as a universal offering being the ultimate ransom paid for the total remission of sins to each and every accepting person of all Mankind.

To: Pmary65 (Quote Begins)

"What you have indicated is that a sabbath was the true original day for the Lord's resurrection. If this was the case as you have explained it, how then was it that the eighth day known as SUNDAY and as the first day of the week did become the mainstream staple for Christian weekly worship? " (Quote Ends)

From 'The Free Republic' forum (The Resurrection on One of the Sabbaths?) as posted on Monday, June 08, 2009 8:18:05 AM by Langel

To: Langel,

By: Pmary65 - William R Priebe (Quotes Begin)

" The Book of Acts shows in numerous places that the Apostles met and continued to meet for worship on the Sabbath days. This appears to have been the norm as shown elsewhere in the New Testament. There is not one indication showing otherwise when you read and identify the scriptures as it is preserved consistently through the original Greek texts."

"History shows that after the fall of Jerusalem (AD~69), Judeo-Christian practices were suppressed and dissolved under the influences of the early Caesars permeating to an all time low."

"A new premise for Christians eventually opened up under the campaign of Emperor 'Constantine the Great' (AD~288–337)."

" In his civil reign, governing magistrates complied with legislated Sunday observance (AD~321) in all of the Roman Empire."

" New considerations followed for Christians by the singular established Church-State formation giving organization to a string of Church councils. A formal introductory gathering of bishops at Arles (AD~317), and Nicaea (AD 325) countered the Easter debate. This paved the way for treatise and established Church Canons at the Edict of Laodicea (AD~364) giving further state tolerance to Christians living along side the pagan worshipers to the deity of Mithraism and the monotheistic Sol Invictus cult."

"The Church historian 'Eusebius of Caesarea' (AD~325) was a rallying contender in aid to the newly formed Christian campaign having his hands in it in several ways. He was a magnificent scholar with possession of the early Church library which has raised suspicion that he may have edited bible writings of earlier Church Leaders to deceive Christian readers into recognition of his Emperor's new found claims in justification for Sunday Church worship."

"Although such allegations are difficult to prove, Eusebius may have acted as an Interpolater to forge parts of documents written by earlier writers such as Barnabas (AD~100), Ignatius (AD~107), Justin Martyr (AD~147), and Irenaeus (AD~175) where various statements were made in reference to the 'resurrection' occurring on the 'first day', the 'eighth day' and 'Sunday'." (Quotes End)

*Here we have Eusebius' account of Constantine speaking of unanimity regarding Easter against the practice of the Jews; (Quotes Begin)

"At the meeting (Nicaea) the question concerning the most holy day of Easter was discussed, and it was resolved by the united judgment of all present, that the feast ought to be kept by all in every place on one and the same day...For we have it in our power, if we abandon their (Jewish) custom, to prolong the due observance of this ordinance to future ages, by a truer (Imperial) order, which we have preserved from the very day of passion until the present time. Let us have nothing in common with the detestable Jewish crowd; for we have received from our Saviour a different way." (Quotes End)

'Eusebius': The Life of Constantine Chapter XVIII

From the Nicene and Post-Nicene Fathers of the Christian Church (Volume 1)

by Philip Schaff; WM. B. Eerdmans Publishing Company, Grand Rapids, 1956

***

The Epistle of the Emperor Constantine, Concerning the matters transacted at the Council (Nicaea), addressed to those Bishops who were not present; (Quotes Begin)

Constantine Augustus to the churches;

" I now proceed briefly to recapitulate the whole of the preceding. The judgment of all is, that the holy pascal feast should be held on one and the same day ; for, in so holy a matter, it is not right that difference of custom should prevail. It is the more commendable to obey this decree, because it precludes all association with error and with sin. This being the case, receive with gladness the heavenly gift and sacred command; for all that is transacted in the holy councils of the bishops, is sanctioned by the Divine will.

Therefore, when you have made known to all our beloved brethren the subject of the epistle, you will be bound to conform to the regular observance of this holy day, so that when, according to my long cherished desire, I shall be with you, I may be able to celebrate with you this holy festival upon one and the same day..." (Quotes End)

Reiterated by Theodoretus Bishop of Cyrus (AD 387~AD 458)

The Greek Ecclesiastical Historians of The First Six Centuries of The Christian Era. Book I Chapter X 'Esuebius's Life of Constantine' by Samuel Bagster & Sons, London, 1845

***

Constantine speaking at Nicaea; (Quotes Begin)

"Since, therefore, it was needful that this matter should be rectified, so that we might have nothing in common with that nation of parricides who slew their Lord: and since that arrangement is consistent with propriety which is observed by all of the churches of the western, southern, and northern parts of the world, and by some eastern also: for these reasons all are unanimous on this present occasion in thinking it worthy of adoption." (Quotes End)

'Eusebius': The Life of Constantine Chapter XIX

From the Nicene and Post-Nicene Fathers of the Christian Church Volume 1 Philip Schaff; WM. B. Eerdmans Publishing Company, Grand Rapids, 1956

* Constantine: The Lord's Day and Day of Preparation Eusebius speaks; (Quotes Begin)

"He ordained, too, that one day should be regarded as a special occasion for prayer: I mean that which is truly the first and chief of all, the day of our Lord and Saviour...Accordingly he enjoined all the subjects of the Roman empire to observe the Lord's day, as a day of rest, and also to honour the day which precedes the Sabbath; in memory, I suppose, of what the Saviour of mankind is recorded to have achieved on that day. And since his desire was to teach his whole army zealously to honour the Saviour's day which derives its name from light and from the sun."

(Quotes End)

Eusebius, The Life of Constantine, Book iv, Chapter xviii, From the Nicene and Post – Nicene Fathers of the Christian Church Volume 1 Philip Schaff; WM. B. Eerdmans Publishing Company, Grand Rapids, 1956

GREEK CLARIFICATION ON TWO SEPARATELY

DEFINED MEANINGS:

(Quotes Begin)

"First of the Sabbaths" is a mistranslation of the Greek. The word μία, "one," is feminine, and must agree with the (understood) feminine word ημέρα, "day." The word Σάββατον (plural Σάββατα), on the other hand, is neuter. In Greek, "first of the Sabbaths" would have to be πρωτον των Σαββάτων, and "one of the Sabbaths" would have to be εν των

Σαββάτων. Μία των Σαββάτων means "(day) one of the Sabbaths," i.e. of a seven-day period from one Sabbath to the next. See Liddell/Scott/Jones' authoritative Greek – English Lexicon s.v. Σάββατον."

(Quotes End) by Bill Berg23 (Moderator) 25/12/06 – from the 'Greek Translatum Forum'.

* Note - In Greek; σ = s and Σ = S.

* Note - Here we have an idiomatic understanding that reckons Civil calendar week (days) in a numerical order from Sabbath to Sabbath.

* Note - Here however, the word 'day' from 'ημέρα' is non-existent in the original Greek N.T. resurrection passages and has been added later to all of the translated verses to make an implied meaning for 'the first day of the week' as representing Sunday.

*Here we have a description defining the various Sabbaths. (Quotes Begin)

"The actual translation is "MIA TWN SABBATWN". Sabbaton is not Sabbatwn." "Sabbaton is the invented Greek word for Sabbath (the Greeks had no such word...or day). Sabbatwn is also an invented Greek word meaning "Special Sabbath". If you look at the link you'll notice that in each case where the word Sabbatwn is used it designates either an Annual Sabbath (one of God's seven) or it designates one of the seven Special Sabbaths between Passover and Pentecost."

"All of the resurrection passages use the word Sabbatwn, not Sabbaton. These are [Matthew 28:1][Mark 16:2] [Luke 24:1] and [John 20:1]. In addition you'll also notice the word Sabbatwn describing the Sabbath in

[Acts 20:7] and [I Corinthians 16:2] which are verses always included in an incorrect attempt to prove up a Sunday resurrection. If it is a normal Sabbath being referenced the New Testament will use the word Sabbaton, Sabbasin......or if the word Sabbath is an adjective (like in Sabbath day) it will be Sabbatou. Sabbtw is the singular form of Sabbatwn."

"The word Sabbaton is derived from the Hebrew and the associated words in the link come from the Hebrew also. Here is [Leviticus 23:32] describing the "Day of Atonement" from The Tanakh [32 šabat šabātwōn hû' lākem wə'innîtem 'et-nafəšōtêkem bətišə'â lahōdeš bā'ere mē'ere 'ad-'ere tišəbətû šabatəkem: f] This is the Hebrew with English script and pronunciation...obviously."

"As you can see.....the Apostles attempted to transliterate the same sound of Sabatwon (Hebrew) into Sabbatwn (Greek) when referencing a "Special Sabbath" and you also find this usage in the Septuagint as well."

"SABBATWN in the Greek is never used to describe an ordinary Sabbath.....only the Sabbath on which the resurrection occurred or an annual Sabbath.... (e.g.) "one of seven."

(Quotes End) 'Quoted' from Diego1618 (The Resurrection on one of the Sabbaths?) in the 'Free Republic' forum on Friday, June 05, 2009.

*Note here in a biblical understanding that recognizes annual or weekly Sabbaths as they occur within a heptad (a group of seven) fashion.

To view online samples of the 'sabbaton' Koine Greek References visit;

http://www.htmlbible.com/sacrednamebiblecom/kjvstrongs/CONGRK4
52.htm#S4521

* The logic behind this thesis can be derived when deciphering the
Lord's Day passages literally from the original Koine Greek Texts.

* All the Greek source 'sabbaton' text references that were illustrated in
this works complied to:

– THE NEW TESTAMENT IN THE ORINGINAL GREEK by BROOK FOSS
WESTSCOTT & FENTON JOHN ANTHONY HORT by MACMILLAN
COMPANY LIMITED 1885

H KAINH : THE GREEK TESTAMENT by OXFORD CLARENDON PRESS 1905

GREEK NEW TESTAMENT by the UNITED BIBLE SOCIETIES 1966

II Timothy 3:16

"All scripture is given by inspiration of God, and is profitable for doctrine, for reproof, for correction, for instruction in righteousness."

Part B The Breakdown of Evidence:

Sec. 2 Preceding the Passion Period

I would like to appeal to those who esteem one day more than the other. (i.e. Rom14:5)

" One man esteemeth one day above another: another esteemeth every day alike. Let every man be fully persuaded in his own mind."

* Here we shall present a time frame to those who firmly believe that Passover occurred on a Friday Nisan 14th where our Lord may have resurrected on a Sunday Nisan 16th. Here the verse St. John 12:1 would apply as follows;

1. "Then Jesus (Yehoshua) six days (Saturday Nisan 8th) before the Passover (Friday Nisan 14th) came to Bethany (an old location just outside the east temple gate), where Lazarus was, which had been dead, whom he raised from the dead."

(St. John Ch.12 con't...)

"On the next day (Sunday Nisan 9th) much people that were come to the feast, when they heard that Jesus (Yehoshua) was coming to Jerusalem,"

"Took branches of palm trees, and went forth to meet him, and cried, Hosanna: Blessed is the King of Israel that cometh in the name of the Lord."

The likeliness here of our Lord traveling from Jericho (Mth 20:29 ; Luk 19:1) some 14 miles away leading the disciples on route to Bethany arriving on a Sabbath rest day (Sat Nisan 8th) in a traditionally accepted time line was unlikely to have happened i.e. Sabbath's day journey as prescribed in Joshua 3:3,4.

* Now we shall present a day by day chronology leading up to Yehoshua's last Passover for those who esteem a crucifixion event occurring on a Wednesday Nisan 14th with a (3 days & 3 nights) time duration between a Saturday Nisan 17th resurrection. Here combined are the scriptural accounts to reveal that a crucifixion on a Passover of Wednesday Nisan 14th was likely not feasible.

The Gospel of St. John Chapter 12;

1. "Then Jesus (Yehoshua) six days (Thursday Nisan 8th) before the Passover (Wednesday Nisan 14th) came to Bethany, where Lazarus was, which had been dead, whom He raised from the dead."

12. "On the next day (Friday Nisan 9th) much people that were come to the feast, when they heard that Jesus (Yehoshua) was coming to Jerusalem,"

13. "Took branches of palm trees, and went forth to meet him, and cried, Hosanna: Blessed is the King of Israel that cometh in the name of the Lord."

St. Mark Chapter 11 (Friday Nisan 9th)

7. "And they brought the colt to Jesus (Yehoshua), and cast their garments on Him; and He sat upon him."

8. "And many spread their garments in the way: and others cut down branches off the trees, and strewed them in the way."

9. "And they that went before, and they that followed, cried, saying, Hosanna; Blessed is He that cometh in the name of the Lord."

11. "And Jesus (Yehoshua) entered into Jerusalem, and into the temple: and when he had looked round about upon all things, and now the eventide was come, he went out unto Bethany with the twelve."

12 "And on the morrow (Saturday Nisan 10th), when they had come from Bethany, he was hungry:"

15 "And they come to Jerusalem: and Jesus (Yehoshua) went into the temple, and began to cast out them that sold and bought in the temple,

and overthrew the tables of the moneychangers, and the seats of them that sold doves;"

The overall point here is that the day of procurement on Nisan 10 as prescribed in Exodus 12:1-6 occurs in this Gospel time frame on a weekly 7th day Saturday Sabbath. The likeliness of working, and purchasing with money handlers on a Sabbath day was legally forbidden and surely quashed back in the day when the Sanhedrin council governed the sacred calendar.

Merchants on a secular day likely traded with acceptance in the outer courts of the temple only. On the day of procurement (Nisan 10th) lambs without spot or blemish were acquired by buyers with a likely certification by priests for a small fee. Some priests may have been too critical in their examinations taking advantage by requesting more monies for a passed inspection thus being an act of bribery well committed. Vendors may have taken an advantage of buyers as well by raising the prices of lambs which were in high demand as a requirement for the Passover sacrifice.Thus being the probable reasons for Yehoshua to condemn such trading practices.

The author of St. John makes the distinction between Nisan 8 being 'six days before the Passover' (i.e. Nisan 14) in Jhn 12:1, and with Nisan 14 being the day 'before the feast (i.e. Nisan 15-21) of Passover' in Jhn 13:1 when comparing the chronological details consecutively.

** In my opinion both time frames where a Passover Nisan 14th was either on a Friday or on a Wednesday suggest that the precluding time intervals one way or the other just don't lead up correctly for a Passion narrative to follow.

The Old Testament book in Exodus 12:1-6. (Nisan 10th / Nisan 14th) describes how the preparation of the Passover event was to be fulfilled;

1. "And the LORD spake unto Moses and Aaron in the land of Egypt saying,"

2. "This month shall be unto you the beginning of months: it shall be the first month (Nisan) of the year to you."

3. "Speak ye unto all the congregation of Israel, saying, In the tenth (10th) day of this month they shall take to them every man a lamb, according to the house of their fathers, a lamb for an house:"

4. "And if the household be too little for the lamb, let him and his neighbor next unto his house take it according to the number of the souls; every man according to his eating shall make your count for the lamb."

5. "Your lamb shall be without blemish, a male of the first year: ye shall take it out from the sheep, or from the goats:"

6. "And ye shall keep it up until the fourteenth (14th) day of the same month: and the whole assembly of the congregation of Israel shall kill (slaughter) it in the evening (late afternoon before sundown)."

Sec. 3 The Timing of the Passover Meal

The Wednesday or Friday belief has associated the last supper as a (genuine?) Passover meal beginning on the night of Nisan 14th prior the following afternoon where 'Josephus' describes the Passover lambs being slain and prepared by pilgrims who had attended the feast.

In the early Nisan 14th context it would then appear that the setting was an ordinary common meal as described in St. John 13:1-2 'before the feast' and NOT an event of a ceremonial Passover Seder as prepared for later from Matthew 26:17; Mark 14:12, Luke 22:7 when our Lord and disciples met on the late afternoon of Nisan 14th 'WHEN THE HOUR HAD COME' & 'I HAVE DESIRED TO EAT THIS PASSOVER WITH YOU' (Luk 22:14,15) where the roasted lamb followed 'AND AS THEY SAT AND DID EAT' (Mrk 14:18) in the nightly beginning of Nisan 15th on the 'first day of unleavened bread'. See Exodus 12:8.

* In my proposing Passion chronology the 'last supper' probably surpassed the Passover Seder partaken on the nightly beginning of Friday Nisan 15th (N.T.) and was likely carried over to the nightly beginning of Monday Nisan 18th in the 'Didascalia Apostolorum' where Yehoshua was finally apprehended and held for examination by the various critical authorities.

"Then led they Jesus (Yehoshua) from Caiaphas unto the hall of judgment: and it was early; and they themselves went not into the judgment hall, lest they should be defiled; but that they might eat the passover." (i.e. St. John 18:28).

 * Note – This precautionary gesture should not have been a ritual concern to the priests if this scene had occurred earlier on the secular

day of Nisan 14th being a preparation day of ceremonial non-cleanliness prior to the actual feast.

However, the Passover feast lasted for seven days (Nisan 15th – 21st) and it was a priestly concern to not be disqualified (on any one of those days) by fulfilling the requirement carefully to the purification laws strictly for the remaining entire duration.

Consider as well the tractrate Sanhedrin – 4:1 from (AD~200) which specifies the explicit times reserved for capital cases regarding trial matters likely in effect of long standing since the days of Yehoshua's Passion;

"They hold the trial during the daytime...and the verdict must also be reached during the daytime...a verdict of conviction not until the following day. Therefore trials may not be held on the eve of the Sabbath, or on the eve of a (high Sabbath) festival day..." (Quotes End)

The Mishna, Herbert Danby, Hendrickson Publishers, 1933 Pg. 387

It is apparent that the whole council met on the morning in the Gospel narrative as shown in Mark 15:1. If this was the day of the actual trial, the conviction then must have occurred on a later day as reasoned from John 19:16.

Therefore, either a 'Friday' or a 'Wednesday' last supper with a mock trial all on Nisan 14th prior to a High Sabbath of Nisan 15th falls short in a time line to the Sanhedrin judicial requirements.

The same reasoning follows on the contrary to those who support the hypothesis of a crucifixion event occurring on a Friday Nisan 15th. Such legal procedures on consecutive days must have been held on secularized days within the Passover feast-period only.

If the Didascalia Apostolorum (AD~290) were correct in conveying the 'apprehension' occurring on the nightly beginning of the fourth day (of the Passover feast) then the trial continued later on that same day being Monday Nisan 18th.

Thus the Sanhedrin conviction must have occurred on the fifth day being on Tuesday Nisan 19th.

Pilate's submission allowing the crucifixion event would have followed on Wednesday Nisan 20th being the stated preparation (secular) day prior to the high solemn sabbath of Thursday Nisan 21st being the last final feast day (Holy Convocation day) of the Passover period.

Sec. 4 The Traditional Passover Account

* The events of a Passover meal (a commemoration of the 'Exodus') in relation to the 'Last Supper' (the indoctrination of the New Covenant) appears simultaneous in the timing as the Gospels reveal. However there remains much debate amongst theologians as to when the actual timing of these events occurred. To remain objective let us refer to an earlier finding to support the latter. The Historian Josephus (AD~70) gives an account of the great preparation leading up to the Exodus; (Quotes Begin)

"But when God had signified, that with one more plague he would compel the Egyptians to let the Hebrews go, he commanded Moses to tell the people that they should have a sacrifice ready, and they should prepare themselves on the tenth month Xanthicus, against the fourteenth (which month is called by the Egyptians Pharmuth, and Nisan [= first month e.g. Esther 3:7] by the Hebrews; but the Macedonians call it Xanthicus) and that he should carry away the Hebrews with all that they had. Accordingly, he having got the Hebrews ready for their departure, and having sorted the peoples into tribes, he kept them together in one place; but when the fourteenth day was come, and all were ready to depart, they offered the sacrifice, and purified their houses with the blood, using hyssop for that purpose; and when they had supped they burnt the remainder of the flesh, as just ready to depart." (Quotes End)

Antiquities of the Jews Book 2, Chapter 14, Paragraph 6. William Whiston

* If Yehoshua's last supper was a 'genuine Passover Seder' on the nightly beginning of Nisan 14th as many purport how then was it a ritual commemorating the Israelites who ate it in haste (Ex 12:11) before fleeing from Egypt on Nisan 15th?

"And they departed from Rameses in the first month, on the fifteenth day of the first month; on the morrow of the Passover the children of Israel went out with a high hand in the sight of all the Egyptians." – Numbers 33:3

Furthermore... (Quote Begins)

"They left Egypt in the month of Xanthicus, on the fifteenth day of the lunar month; four hundred and thirty years after our forefather Abraham came into Canaan, but two hundred and fifteen years only after Jacob removed unto Egypt." (Quote Ends)

Antiquities of the Jews Book 2 Chapter 15, Paragraph 2. William Whiston – 1998 Thomas Nelson Publishers

Also...(Quote Begins)

"Remember the commandment which the Lord commanded thee concerning the Passover, that thou shouldst celebrate it in it's season on the fourteenth of the first month, that thou shouldst kill it before its evening, and that they should eat it by night on the evening of the fifteenth from the time of the setting of the sun." (Quote Ends) Jubilees 49:1 (160~BC) Translated by Robert H. Charles, 1914

See Online at;http://www.summascriptura.com/html/Jubilees_RHC.html

Why would the Israelites in Moses' time have to wait around for at least 24 hours after eating a meal in haste on the beginning of Nisan 14th before departing from Egypt on the next night of Nisan 15th?

"Observe the month of Abib (Nisan), and keep the Passover unto the Lord thy God; for in the month of Abib the Lord thy God brought thee forth out of Egypt by night."

Deuteronomy 16:1

The verse says; ' out of Egypt by night' thus indicating a most precarious time when darkness and moonlight was upon them.

If the Israelites in Moses' time did eat the Passover meal in the beginning of Nisan 14th (as many theologians persist), then it should stand to reason that they could have departed 'in haste' (fully assembled-fully prepared) that very night, shortly afterwards. However, the Bible account and Josephus' account clearly agree together that the Israelites began to leave in the night of Nisan 15th some short time later after eating the meal.

Likewise our Lord's Passover (lamb) meal was kept as prescribed on the nightly beginning of Nisan 15th. That moment was known as a high annual Sabbath (signifying Israel's departure from Egypt) or a 'Yom Tov" (Hebrew) meaning as 'Good Day' which later became traditionally known to Christians as 'Good Friday'. 'Good Friday' not because Yehoshua died, on that day. Think about it, what is good about someone being crucified to death? It was good because an invocation by our Lord Yehoshua was offered and made personal to all believers through his shared intimate moments where the allotted elements at that Seder table were combined systematically through Him being consecrated into a life eternal preserving sustenance. Hear the words from the Apostle Paul "For even Christ our Passover is sacrificed (consecrated) for us" (1 Cor 5:7) rings true on the night of the Passover Seder.

The turning of the biblical events that unfolded afterwards becomes almost immeasurable. One account indicates a prior intention to not press matters against Yehoshua 'Not on a feast Day' as noted in Matthew 26:5 and Mark 14:2. However, another account at Mark 15:6 and Luke 23:17 shows that the crucifixion moment did succumb to being 'ON A FEAST DAY' within the Passover period. Over the years I have become aware of the various positions by theologians as to 'WHEN' the last supper, the crucifixion, and the resurrection moments occurred. Opinions and beliefs are strongly divided. Church official authorities opt to a more passive stance admitting that such historical details to this day remain a 'mystery'.

Why did these important events regardless of when they happened as recorded from our history did come to pass? What remains significant from those events that has carried us on through the ages into a modern day existence with a stake of it in our own individual lives? Only you can answer that question, the answer is in your heart, you have your conviction, and I have mine.

Sec. 5 Clarifying the Passion Passover Narrative

Here is a statement from the late Dr. William Brown D.D. (Quotes Begin)

"We are therefore come, in strict propriety of speech, to the beginning of the fifteenth day; for we formerly saw, that the Jewish manner of computing time was from sunsetting to sunsetting. The Paschal lamb, therefore, although it was killed on the fourteenth day of the month, was not eaten till the beginning of the fifteenth; for it was killed between three o'clock in the afternoon and sunset, but was not eaten till after sunset."

(Quotes End) Antiquities of the Jews and Their Customs Illustrated, Vol.I, Part IV, Sec.I – William Brown D.D. Published by William D. Woodward, Philadelphia 1823

* Note – Therefore in the event of Yehoshua eating the Passover at the designated time, the crucifixion must have followed later on a secular (preparation) day by where traveling, work, and purchasing were not legally prohibited by Jewish law as shown in Mark chapter 15. (Quotes Begin)

21. "And they compelled one Simon a Cyrenian, who passed by, coming out of the country, the father of Alexander and Rufus, to bear His cross."

42. "And now when the even was come, because it was the preparation, that is, the day before the sabbath."

46. "And he bought fine linen, and took Him down, and wrapped Him in the linen, and laid Him in a sepulchre which was hewn out of a rock, and rolled a stone unto the door of the sepulchre." (Mark Quotes End)

Such secular activities occurring on a Friday Nisan 15th (High Sabbath) afternoon would be solemnly improbable and forbidden under Jewish law. More time was also required for the earlier events of Yehoshua being present with Annas, Caiaphas, Herod Antipas, with three reproaches by Pilate (Luk 23:22), and placed before the vast throngs of peoples on a couple occasions. These events could not have easily compacted within a narrow time line of about 16 hours or less, for a night time mock trial, judgment sentencing, crucifixion (i.e. Mrk 15:25) along with the burial preparations of Yehoshua. However, all of these secular activities spread proportionately over a couple days leading up to a Wednesday Nisan 20th (preparation day) before a solemn Thursday Nisan 21st High Sabbath was very plausible.

Most Christians may associate the Passion narrative subconsciously occurring in the year AD 33 where the numbers 33 are synonymous to the numbers in the prophecy of '3 days and 3 nights' as stated in Matthew 12: 39, 40.

* Note – If Yehoshua died on an afternoon of a Friday the day immediately prior to the weekly Saturday Sabbath with a resurrection on an early Sunday morning, the literal resurrection phrase 'one of the sabbaths' translated from the Koine Greek becomes an idiomatic expression. The time duration in the grave would be about 36 hours, and barely not enough time to quantify for the 'only sign' given as warranted through the Old Testament model of Jonah.

"Now the LORD had prepared a great fish to swallow up Jonah. And Jonah was in the belly of the fish three days and three nights." Jonah 1:17

"A wicked and adulterous generation seeketh after a sign; and there shall no sign be given unto it, but the sign of the prophet Jonah. And he left them, and departed." Matthew 16:4

"But he (Yehoshua) answered and said unto them, An evil and adulterous generation seeketh after a sign, and there will be no sign be given to it, but the sign of the prophet, Jonah; For as Jonah was three days and three nights in the belly of the great fish, so shall the Son of man be three days and three nights in the heart of the earth." Matthew 12:39, 40

Subsequently, the 'sign of Jonah' phrase of 'three days and three nights' as 'no sign given but' became less understood and commonly avoided by many scholars to the least justification in biblical relevance.

"And when the people were gathered thick together, He began to say, This is an evil generation: they seek a sign; and there shall no sign be given it, but the sign of Jonah the prophet." Luke 11:29

Compare also 'The Didascalia Apostolorum' (AD~230) which states;

"The Son of Man must pass three days and three nights."

Compare also to 'The Apostolic Constitutions of the Holy Fathers' (AD~375) where it reads; "The Son of man must continue in the heart of the earth three days and three nights."

Consider turning the phrase around to show as 'three nights and three days'. This order may fit truer to a Jewish reckoning in perspective of Hebrew time.

Many traditional theologians will rationalize Jews regarding a little bit of a day in an inclusive counting being equivalent to a whole day, however, Yehoshua stated quite clearly; "Are there not twelve hours (daylight) in a day? " St. John 11:9

Technically a total of 36 hours of daylight can be accounted for between the burial and resurrection moment.

Hence with; Wednesday Nisan 20th (last 1 hour), Thursday Nisan 21 (12 hours), Friday Nisan 22 (12 hours), and Saturday Nisan 23 (11 hours) are combined to a total length of 36 hours. As well, 3 nights of darkness can be accounted for by; Thursday Nisan 21 (4 watches), Friday Nisan 22 (4 watches), and Saturday Nisan 23 (4 watches) where the sunset of night was the beginning of each new daily calendar period.

* Here we have 'The Paschal Feast and The Lord's Supper' as stated by the late Rev. Dr. Alfred Edersheim (Quotes Begin)

" In attempting an accurate chronology of these days it must always be remembered that the Passover was sacrificed between the evenings of the 14th and the 15th of Nisan ; that is, before the close of the 14th and the beginning of the 15th. The Paschal Supper, however took place on the 15th itself (that is according to Jewish reckoning – the day beginning as the first stars became visible)."

(Quotes End) 'The Temple, Its Ministry and Services as they were At The Time Of Jesus [Yehoshua] Christ' 1874 Chapter XI 'The Passover' Rev. Dr. Alfred Edersheim

* Further more...(Quotes Continue)

"So important is it to have a clear understanding of all that passed on that occasion, that at the risk of some repetition, we shall now attempt to piece together the notices in the various Gospels, adding to them again those explanations which have just been given in detail. At the onset we may dismiss, an unworthy of serious discussion, the theory, either that our Lord had observed the Paschal Supper at another than the regular time for it, or that St. John meant to indicate that He had partaken of it on the 13th instead of the 14th of Nisan."

"To such violent hypothesis, which are wholly uncalled for,there is this one conclusive answer, that except on the evening of the 14th of Nisan, no Paschal lamb could have been offered in the temple, and therefore no Paschal Supper celebrated in Jerusalem."

(All Quotes End) The Temple, Its Ministry and Services as they were At The Time Of Jesus (Yehoshua) Christ. 1874 Chapter XII 'The Paschal Feast And The Lord's Supper, Rev. Dr. Alfred Edersheim

Sec.7 Clarifying the Old Testament Passover Review

* Many believers identify that 'Christ our Passover' and the 'Lamb of God' pertains directly to a crucifixion event being linked to the time when the Passover lambs were being slain. Many have associated the timing for Yehoshua's crucifixion to the public sacrifice on the Passover late afternoon of Nisan 14th. It is not then any wonder why Yehoshua's Passover supper occurring later in the next nightly beginning on the first day (Nisan 15th) of unleavened bread gets totally misconstrued. To them who think it was essential that He be crucified while lambs were being slain consider that such activities were carried forward on a daily basis by the temple priests for each and every remaining day of the Passover feast period.

Numbers Chapter 28

Numbers 28:3 "And thou shalt say unto them, this is the offering made by fire which ye shall offer unto the LORD; two lambs of the first year without spot day by day, for a continual burnt offering."

Numbers 28:4 "The one lamb shalt thou offer in the morning [dawn], and the other lamb shalt thou offer at *even."

(i.e. lit. 'between two evenings' = the period of time between the sun's descending point in the skies meridian at 3:00 p.m. whilst settling through twilight at 5:00 p.m. with the sun hidden over the horizon in the day's closing of darkness at 6:00 p.m. near the Vernal Equinox). See also; Ex 12:6.

Numbers 28:16 "And in the fourteenth day of the first month (Abib/Nisan) is the Passover of the LORD."

Numbers 28:17 "And in the fifteenth day of this month is the feast: seven days shall unleavened bread be eaten."

Numbers 28:18 "In the first day (Nisan 15) shall be a holy convocation; ye shall do no manner of servile work therein:"

Numbers 28:19 "But ye shall offer a sacrifice made by fire for a burnt offering unto the LORD; two young bullocks, and one ram, and seven lambs of the first year: they shall be unto you without blemish:"

Numbers 28:20 "And their meat offering shall be of flour mingled with oil: three tenth deals shall ye offer for a bullock, and two tenth deals for a ram;"

Numbers 28:21 "A several tenth deal shalt thou offer for every lamb, throughout the seven lambs:"

Numbers 28:22 "And one goat for a sin offering to make atonement for you."

Numbers 28:23 "Ye shall offer these beside the burnt offering in the morning, which is for a continual burnt offering."

Numbers 28:24 "After this manner ye shall offer daily, throughout the seven days, the meat of the sacrifice made by fire, of a sweet savoir unto the LORD: it shall be offered beside the continual burnt offering, and his drink offering."

Numbers 28:25 "And on the seventh (Nisan 21) day ye shall have a holy convocation ye shall do no servile work."

* We can see from Numbers 28:24 that a daily sacrifice of lambs were offered by temple priests on the remaining seven days of the Passover period. Each day two young bullocks, one ram, and seven lambs of the first year, and one goat were sacrificed along with the daily sacrifice of two young lambs for the morning and the evening ritual. These sacrifices were inclusive after the public sacrifice on Nisan 14th for the full remaining seven days of the Passover feast period.

Exodus 12:6 "And ye shall keep it (the Passover lamb) up until the fourteenth day of the same month: and the whole assembly of the congregation of Israel shall kill it in the evening (i.e. between two evenings)."

Exodus 12:18 "In the first month, on the fourteenth day of the month at even, ye shall eat unleavened bread, until the one and twentieth day of the month at even."

Leviticus 23:6 "And on the fifteenth day of the same month is the feast of unleavened bread unto the LORD: seven days ye must eat unleavened bread."

.

Thus the above passages are to be understood as follows;

1) Sunset on Nisan 14 to sunset on Nisan 15 equals the 1st day of unleavened bread.

2) Sunset on Nisan 15 to sunset on Nisan 16 equals the 2nd day of unleavened bread.

3) Sunset on Nisan 16 to sunset on Nisan 17 equals the 3rd day of unleavened bread.

4) Sunset on Nisan 17 to sunset on Nisan 18 equals the 4th day of unleavened bread.

5) Sunset on Nisan 18 to sunset on Nisan 19 equals the 5th day of unleavened bread.

6) Sunset on Nisan 19 to sunset on Nisan 20 equals the 6th day of unleavened bread.

7) Sunset on Nisan 20 to sunset on Nisan 21 equals the 7th day of unleavened bread.

After carefully reviewing the Old Testament scriptures, you will see that the Passover lamb was slaughtered by Jews on Passover Nisan 14 in the late afternoon when the sun was setting down. The roasted Passover lamb was then consecrated with unleavened bread a short time later on the nightly beginning of Nisan 15. That as a night to be commemorated continually by Jews as a reminder of the earlier time when their forefathers ate the Seder to purify their souls, and preserved their posterity by the marked blood of the lamb. As a ritual of gratitude to God almighty where any remains of the Passover lamb were to be sacrificed and thoroughly consumed by fire before the Nisan 15th morning. (i.e. Ex 12:10)

Sec. 8 Clarifying the New Testament Passover Review

* Note – I have taken the liberty to clarify meanings as shown in the supplemented round (brackets).

St. Matthew follows;

26:2 "Ye know that after two days is the feast of the passover (Nisan 15 – 21), and the Son of man is betrayed (plotted) to be crucified."

26:17 "Now (anticipating) the first day (Nisan 15) of the feast of unleavened bread the disciples came to Jesus (Yehoshua), saying unto him, Where wilt thou that we prepare (Nisan 14) for thee to eat (Nisan 15) the passover?"

26:18 "And He said, Go into the city to such a man, and say unto him, Thy Master saith, My time is at hand; I will keep the passover at thy house with my disciples."

26:19 "And the disciples did as Jesus (Yehoshua) appointed them; and they made ready the passover."

26:20 "Now when the even was come (in the end of Nisan 14 and the nightly beginning of Nisan 15), He sat down with the twelve."

26:21 "And as they did eat..."

St. Mark follows;

14:1 "After two days was the feast of the Passover (Nisan 14), and of unleavened bread (Nisan 15-21) ..."

* Note – the 'feast' does not literally appear here in the original Greek passage but has been supplanted by the KJV Translators which is subtlety misleading to suggest Nisan 14 as a feast day when in fact of actually it was the preparation day before the feast.

14:12 "And (in anticipation of) the first day (Nisan 15) of unleavened bread, when they killed (sacrificed) the passover, His disciples said un to Him, Where wilt thou that we go and prepare (Nisan 14) that thou mayest eat (Nisan 15) the passover?"

* Note here that there are some irregularities in this two-fold passage. Readers need to realize here that the context is split up in a cross-tense with the preparation of the slaughtered lamb on Nisan 14 (in the present tense) followed by the Passover Seder (yet to happen in the future tense) on the first day of unleavened bread being Nisan 15th when they consecrated (ate), and sacrificed the Passover lamb's remains in fire before morning, i.e. Ex 12:10.

The KJV Translators misconstrued use of the word 'killed' in Mark 14:12 and Luke 22:7 as is incorrect and misleading to displace the 'first day of unleavened bread' event as occurring on Nisan 14 which is totally wrong. More appropriate words there could have read as 'consecrated or sacrificed'.

14:13 "And He sendeth forth two of his disciples, and saith unto them, Go ye into the city, and there shall meet you a man bearing a pitcher of water: follow him."

14:14 "And wheresoever He shall go in, say ye to the good man of the house, The Master saith, Where is the guest chamber, where I shall eat the passover with my disciples?"

14:15 "And He will shew you a large upper room furnished and prepared: there make ready for us."

14:16 "And His disciples went forth, and came into the city, and found as He had said unto them: and they made ready the Passover."

14:17 "And in the evening (in the end of Nisan 14 and the nightly beginning of Nisan 15), He cometh with the twelve."

14:18 "And as they sat and did eat..."

Mark 14:17, 18 is actually describing the fulfillment of the Passover Seder on the beginning of Nisan 15th as instructed in the O.T. time. The same reasoning of using the proper tense(s) follows for the passages of Matthew 26:17 and Luke 22:7. Thus, the lamb was slaughtered on Passover Nisan 14th but was consumed on the nightly beginning of Nisan 15th being on the 'first day of unleavened bread'.

St. Luke follows;

2:41 "Now His parents went to Jerusalem every year at the feast of the passover."

2:42 "And when He was twelve years old, they went up to Jerusalem after the custom of the feast."

22:1 "Now the feast of unleavened bread (Nisan 15-21) drew nigh, which is called the passover."

22:7 "Then came (approaching) the day of unleavened bread (Nisan 15), when the passover must be killed (sacrificed)."

* Note – Again, the lamb was slaughtered on Passover Nisan 14th but was eaten at the nightly Seder beginning on Nisan 15th being the 'first day of unleavened bread'. There it was consumed and any remains were to be destroyed by fire as a sacrifice to the Almighty Heavenly Father. (e.g. Ex 12:10)

22:8 "And he sent Peter and John, saying, Go and prepare us the passover, that we may eat."

22:9 "And they said unto Him, Where wilt thou that we prepare (Nisan 14)?"

22:10 "And he said unto them, Behold, when ye are entered into the city, there shall a man meet you, bearing a pitcher of water; follow him into the house where he entereth in."

22:11 "And ye shall say unto the good man of the house, The Master saith unto thee, Where is the guest chamber, where I shall eat the passover (Nisan 15) with my disciples?"

22:12 "And he shall shew you a large upper room furnished: there make ready."

22:13 "And they went, and found as He had said unto them: and they made ready the passover."

22:14 "And when the hour (e.g. in the twelfth hour about 5:00 p.m. – 6:00 p.m. in the twilight at 'even' being the end of Nisan 14) was come, He sat down, and the twelve apostles with him."

22:15 "And He said unto them, With desire I have desired to eat (e.g. on the nightly beginning of Nisan 15th) this passover with you before I suffer."

22:16 "For I say unto you, I will not any more eat (another feast nor complete the remaining fast of unleavened bread) thereof until it be fulfilled in the kingdom of God."

22:17 "And He took the cup, and gave thanks, and said, Take this, and divide it among yourselves:"

22:18 "For I say unto you, I will not drink of the fruit of the vine (again), until the kingdom of God shall come."

*Note – the Reverend Joachim Jeremias authored a book entitled; 'The Eucharistic Words of Christ' in 1966 by Scribner Co. from The University of California. He believed that the Bible describes 'The Last Supper' (Passover Seder) occurring on the nightly beginning of Nisan 15.

St. John follows;

2:13 "And the Jews' passover was at hand, and Jesus (Yehoshua) went up to Jerusalem."

2:23 "Now when He was in Jerusalem at the passover, in the feast day, many believed in his name, when they saw the miracles which he did."

6:4 "And the Passover, a feast of the Jews (Nisan 15-21), was nigh."

11:55 "And the Jews' passover (Nisan 14) was nigh at hand: and many went out of the country up to Jerusalem before the passover, to purify themselves."

12:1 "Then Jesus (Yehoshua) six days (Friday Nisan 8) before the Passover (Thursday Nisan 14) came to Bethany..."

13:1 "Now (the end of Nisan 14) before the feast (Nisan 15-21) of the passover, when Jesus (Yehoshua) knew that his hour..."

18:28 "Then led they Jesus (Yehoshua) from Caiaphas unto the hall of judgment; and it was early (possibly on Tuesday Nisan 19th); and they themselves went not into the judgement hall, lest they should be defiled; but that they might eat (fulfill completely) the (full duration of the) passover (period)."

18:39 "But ye have a custom, that I should release unto you one at the passover..."

19:14 "And it was the 'preparation' of the passover, and about the sixth hour (12 p.m.): and he (Pilate) saith unto the Jews, Behold your King!"

*Note – Here it says 'preparation' and not 'eve'. The word 'preparation' was commonly used to describe a secular day before a weekly Sabbath or a floating high (annual) Sabbath. If it had said 'eve' then this could have been a reasonable reference to the end of Nisan 14 before Nisan 15 being the first day of the feast. But here it reasonably signifies the preparation day of Nisan 20th before the second high sabbath of Nisan 21st at the end of the Passover feast. Thus, Yehoshua died on a preparation day before the high 'μεγάλη' sabbath as stated in John 19:31. Compare 'μεγάλη' also in John 7:37 describing 'μεγάλη' as a 'high' occasion being the 'last day' in the feast of Tabernacles. See also Luke 2:43 for 'the last day of the feast'.

*Note – A possible time duration between John 13:1 (Thursday 12th hour as 5 – 6 p.m. on Nisan 14th) and John 18:28 (Tuesday 7:00 a.m. Nisan 19) whilst counting days from sunset to sunset would have been about 4.5 days. This time lapse may be accounted for (when comparing details) in other Passion testimonies such as 'The Didascalia Apostolorum' and 'The Apocryphal Gospel of Peter'.

Christian fundamentalism is based ideally on a premise that Yehoshua had to die on the public late afternoon sacrifice of the Nisan 14 Passover, and should have resurrected as a first fruit on the Nisan 16 Jewish sheaf offering day. Merely thus, an incomplete conclusion to scripture omitting the sign of Jonah, where rectified as the only hard evidence, being a priority set standard where all other Passion stated details are fused in line across the board with the fulfilled resurrection prophecy of our Lord Yehoshua.

Sec. 9 The Passion Account from the Apostolic Constitutions of the Holy Fathers

 The Apostolic Constitutions of The Holy Fathers was composed from Greek origin within the fourth century by various Church Leaders and was likely reconstituted from the older written Passion account of the third century Syriac Didascalia Apostolorum.

In contrast, the references regarding the Passion story were reconfigurd in scale to a Civil calendar week but were most likely intended to be understood initially in the consecutive order of feast days as they landed on the Passover period.

 Here I present the chronology in accordance to the revamped Civil calendar week and I have supplemented dates in (brackets) to clarify the Passion Narrative along with a proposed time frame showing that the Passover period at the time of our Lord's Passion appears to have occurred on a Friday Nisan 14th when the full moon fell on the years of either AD 30 or AD33.

The first day (of the Civil calender week) fell on Sunday Nisan 9th, the second day fell on Monday Nisan 10th, the third day fell on Tuesday Nisan 11th, the fourth day fell on Wednesday Nisan 12th, the fifth day fell on Thursday Nisan 13th, the sixth day fell on Friday Nisan 14th, with Saturday Nisan 15th being the seventh day of the Civil week. The meaning for the 'first day' is understood in accordance to Leviticus 23:11 that states; "and he (the priest) shall wave the sheaf before the Lord, to be accepted for you: on the morrow after the sabbath the priest shall wave it." Subsequently the "sabbath" here has been wrongfully perceived by Gentiles as the weekly sabbath where the morrow is always fixed on the Sunday as 'the first day of the week'. (More on this in Chapter 11)

* Note - Jews always regarded Nisan 14th as the Passover eve prior to Nisan 15th being the 'first day' of unleavened bread as not applicable here to this Passion narrative.

The Constitutions of the Holy Fathers, Sec. III Book V Chapter XIV (Quotes Begin)

"For they began to hold a council against the Lord on the second (Monday Nisan 10th) day of the (Civil) week, in the first month, which is Xanthicus (Nisan): and the deliberation continued on the third (Tuesday Nisan 11th) day of the (Civil) week; but on the fourth (Wednesday Nisan 12th) day they determined to take away His life by crucifixion..."

he had been long entrusted with the purse..." "And on the fifth (Thursday Nisan 13th) day of the (Civil) week, when we had eaten the (anticapatory) Passover (unleavened bread = wrong) with Him and when Judas had dipped his hand into the dish, and recieved the sop, and was gone out by night, the Lord said to us: "The hour is come that ye shall be dispersed, and shall leave me alone;"

"...and when they had done the like things to Him there, it being the day of the **preparation** (Friday Nisan 14th), they delivered Him to Pilate the Roman governor, accusing Him of many and great things, none of which they could prove. Whereupon the governor, as out of **patience** with them, said: "I find no cause against Him..."

"And themselves became accusers, and witnesses, and judges, and authors of the sentence, saying, "Crucify Him, crucify Him..."

"But the **executioners** took the Lord of glory and nailed Him to the cross, crucifying Him indeed at the sixth hour (12:00 p.m.), but having received the sentence of His **condemnation** at the third hour (e.g. 9:00 a.m., see also Mark 15:25)..."

"Into Thy hands I commit my spirit," He gave up the ghost, and was buried before sunset in a new sepulcher. But when the first day of the week (one of the sabbaths) dawned He arose from the dead, and fulfilled those things which before His passion He foretold to us, saying:"

"The Son of man must **continue** in the heart of the earth three days (Nisan 14, 15, 16) and three **(interpretational)** nights." And when He was risen (Sunday Nisan 16th) from the dead, He appeared first to Mary Magdalene, and Mary the mother of James, then to Cleopas in the way, and after that to us His disciples, who had fled away for fear of the Jews, but privately were very inquisitive about Him."(Quotes End)

Translated from 'Greek' by William Whiston and revised and reprinted by Irah Chase, D.D.

See; Section III, Book V, Chapters XIII – XX
http://www.ccel.org/ccel/schaff/anf07.ix.vi.iii.html

The Constitutions of the Apostolic Fathers, Sec. III Book V Chapter XVII
(Quotes Begin)

XVII. "It is therefore your duty, brethren, who are redeemed by the
precious blood of Christ, to observe the days of the Passover exactly,
with all care, after the vernal equinox, lest ye be obliged to keep the
memorial of the one passion twice in a year. Keep it once only in a year
for Him that died but once."

"Do not you yourselves compute, but keep it when your brethren of the
circumcision do so: keep it together with them; and if they err in their
computation, be not you concerned."

"Keep your nights of watching in the middle of the days of unleavened
bread. And when the Jews are feasting, do you fast and wail over them,
because on the day of their feast they crucified Christ; and while they
are lamenting and eating unleavened bread in bitterness, do you feast."
(Quotes end)

*Note – An intrusion in text proceeds forth from an Interpolater whose
writings were added at a later time. See 'Primitive Christianity' by
William Whiston. The works of interpolation weave on through the text
to the end of book V as follows; (Quote Begins)

"But no longer be careful to keep the feast with the Jews, for we have
now no communion with them; for they have been led astray in regard
to the calculation itself, which they think they accomplish perfectly, that
they may be led astray on every hand, and be fenced off from the
truth."

"But do you observe carefully the vernal equinox, which occurs on the
twenty-second of the twelfth month, which is Dystros (March),
observing carefully until the twenty-first of the moon, lest the
fourteenth of the moon shall fall on another week, and an error being

committed, you should through ignorance celebrate the passover twice in the year, or celebrate the day of the resurrection of our Lord on any other day than a Sunday..." (Quote Ends)

* See also Chapter XVII
http://www.ccel.org/ccel/schaff/anf07.ix.vi.iii.html

Constitutions of the Holy Fathers – Book V Chapter XVIII. (Quote Begins)

"Do you therefore (How-ever) fast on the days of the Passover, beginning from the second day (Nisan 16th) of the week (feast-period) until the preparation (Nisan 20th), and the Sabbath (Nisan 21st) , six days, making use of only bread, and salt, and herbs, and water for your drink."

(Quote Ends) The text used here in all of the above passages are translated from 'Greek' by William Whiston and was revised and reprinted by Irah Chase, D.D. (D. Appleton & C0. New York 1840).

(Reiterated Quote)

"Keep your nights of watching in the middle of the days of unleavened bread. And when the Jews are feasting, do you fast and wail over them, because on the day of their feast they crucified Christ; and while they are lamenting and eating unleavened bread in bitterness, do you feast."

(Quote Ends) The Constitutions of the Apostolic Fathers, Sec. III Book V Chapter XVII

*Note – Here as stated above in contrast to the revised account is the clearest account of Yehoshua's trial and passion event occurring within the Jewish Passover feast period.

Sec. 10 The Passion Account from the Gospel of St. Peter

Here an exception is allotted to the 'Gospel of St. Peter' (AD~180) in a reference from the second century also known as the 'Akhmim Fragments' at verse 12.

(Quote Begins)

"Now it was the last day of unleavened bread, and many went out of the city returning to their houses, the feast being at an end. And we the twelve disciples of the Lord wept and were in sorrow, and every man withdrew to his house sorrowing for what had come to pass."

(Quote Ends)

H.B. Swete – Translator

☆ Here we have a moment in time when the disciples are in bereavement still waiting at the end of the Passover period for the promise of our Lord to fulfill the 'Sign of Jonah' where He would become resurrected 'after 3 days and 3 nights in the heart of the earth'.

Here we have a surviving composition possibly written by multiple authors where the resurrection event overall is mentioned quite briefly.

These non-Canonical writings may relate to the Gospel narrative in a comparative way but do not wholly support the traditionally believed time frame in a chronological way.

* I have taken the liberty to rearrange the fragments in a chronological order of a timely fashion that will display support for a post Passover feast / resurrection moment. As well, I have supplemented calendar

days and comments in (brackets) to assist in clarifying the Fragment's narrative.

'The Apocryphal Gospel of St. Peter' by Swete, H.B. (Translator) published by Macmillan and Co., 1893

(Quotes Begin)

1."But of the Jews none washed his hands, neither Herod, nor any of His judges; and since they did not choose to wash them, Pilate arose. And then Herod the king commandeth the Lord to be taken, saying unto them, what things soever I commanded you to do unto Him, do ye."

3. "And he delivered Him to the people before the first (the original Greek reads; μια = mia = one) day of unleavened bread, their feast. So they took the Lord and pushed Him as they ran, and said: Let us hail the Son of God, since we have gotten power over Him. And they clothed Him with purple, and set Him on a seat of judgment, saying, Judge righteously, O King of Israel. And one of them brought a crown of thorns and put it on the head of the Lord, and others stood and spat upon His eyes, and others smote His cheeks; others pierced Him with a reed, and some scourged Him saying, With this honour let us honour the Son of God."

* In the original Greek verse 3 reads 'before one of unleavened bread' being in Greek Syntax a partitive genitive case function implying generally to any 'one' setting within the seven day feast of the Passover period. Thus an evening time occurring in the middle of the feast.

2. "Now there stood Joseph, the friend of Pilate and of the Lord; and knowing that they were about to crucify Him, he came to Pilate, and begged the body of the Lord for burial. And Pilate sent to Herod and begged His body; and Herod said, Brother Pilate, even if draweth on; for

it is written in the law that the sun set not on one that hath died by violence."

"And they brought two malefactors, and crucified the Lord in the midst of them; but He held His peace, as in no wise suffering pain. And when they had set up the cross, they placed on it the superscription, This is the King of Israel. And they laid His garments before Him, and parted them, and cast lots upon them. But one of the malefactors upbraided them, saying, We have suffered thus for the ills that we wrought, but this man-what wrong hath He done you in that He became the Saviour of men? And they had indignation against him, and commanded that his legs should not be broken, to the end that he might die in torments."

"Now it was midday (12 p.m. on Wed Nisan 20th) , and darkness overspread all Judea; and they were troubled and distressed lest the sun had set, inasmuch as He was yet alive; it is written for them that the sun set not on one that hath died by violence. And one of them said, Give Him gall to drink with vinegar; and they mixed and gave Him to drink. So they accomplished all things, and filled up their sin upon their head. And many went about with lamps, supposing that it was night; and some fell. And the Lord cried aloud, saying, My power, my power. Thou hast left Me; and having said this He was taken up. And the same hour the veil of the temple of Jerusalem was torn in twain."

"And then they drew the nails from the hands of the Lord, and laid Him upon the earth; and the whole earth was shaken and great fear came upon them. Then the sun shone out and it was found to be the ninth hour (3:00 p.m.). But the Jews rejoiced, and they gave His body to Joseph to bury it, inasmuch as he beheld all the good things that He did. So he took the Lord and washed Him and wrapped Him in linen and brought Him into his own tomb, called Joseph's Garden."

"But the Scribes and Pharisees and elders, being assembled together and hearing that the whole people murmured and beat their breasts, saying, If these exceeding great signs were wrought at His death, see how righteous he was – the elders were afraid and came to Pilate, beseeching him and saying, Deliver to us soldiers, that we may guard His sepulcher for three days, lest His disciples come and steal Him away, and the people suppose that He is risen from the dead, and do us mischief. So Pilate delivered unto them Petronius the centurion with soldiers to guard the tomb; and with them there came elders and scribes to the sepulcher, and all who were together rolled a great stone against the door of the sepulcher; and they spread upon it seven seals, and pitched a tent there and kept guard. Now when it was (early) morning, at the dawning (drawing) of the (High) Sabbath (Thurs Nisan 21st), there came a crowd from Jerusalem and the country round about to see the sepulcher, how it had been sealed."

12.(a) "Now it was the last day of unleavened bread (Thurs Nisan 21st) , and many went out (Fri Nisan 22nd) of the city returning to their houses, the feast (Fri Nisan 15th – Thurs Nisan 21st) being at an end. And we the twelve disciples of the Lord wept and were in sorrow, and every man withdrew to his house sorrowing for what had come to pass."

7. "Then the Jews and the elders and the priests, knowing what evil they had done to themselves, began to bewail and say, Woe to our sins! the judgement is at hand, and the end of Jerusalem. And I wish my fellows was in sorrow, and being wounded at the heart we hid ourselves, for we were sought for by them as malefactors and as minded to burn the temple; and besides all this, we were fasting, and we sat mourning and weeping night and day (Fri Nisan 22nd) until the (weekly) Sabbath (Sat Nisan 23rd)."

11.(a) "Now at dawn on the Lord's Day (Sat Nisan 23rd) Mary Magdalene, a female disciple of the Lord – afraid by reason of the Jews, forasmuch as they were inflamed with wrath, she has not done at the sepulcher of the Lord what women are wont to do for those who die and who are dear to them- took with her her female friends, and came to the sepulcher where He was laid."

* Note – The women came early and loitered part of the day in anticipation of the Lord's promise. (con't) "...And they feared lest the Jews should see them, and they said, although we could not weep and bewail Him on the day when He was crucified, let us do so now at His sepulcher. But who shall roll us away the stone which was laid at the door of the sepulcher, that we may enter in and sit by Him, and do the things that are due? for the stone was great, and we fear lest any man see us. And if we cannot, even though we should cast at the door the things which we bring for memorial of Him, we will weep and bewail Him until we come to our house."

"Now on the night (Sat Nisan 23rd) when the Lord's Day (Lord of the Sabbath) was drawing on, as the soldiers kept guard by two and two in a watch, there was a great voice in heaven, and they saw the heavens opened, and two men descend from thence with much light and draw nigh unto the tomb. And the stone which had been cast at the door rolled away of itself and entered in. the soldiers, therefore, when they saw it, awakened the centurion and the elders (for they were also there keeping watch); and as they told the things that they had seen, again they see three men coming forth from the tomb, two of them supporting the other, and a cross following them; and the head of the two reached to heaven, bit that of Him who was led by them overpassed the heavens. And they heard a voice from the heavens, saying, Thou didst preach to them that sleep; and a response was heard from the cross, Yea."

10.(a) "They took counsel therefore with one another to go and shew these things unto Pilate. And while they yet thought on this, the heavens again appeared to open, and a man descended and entered into the sepulcher. When they saw this they of the centurion's company, hastened by night to Pilate."

11.(b) "So they (the women) went and found the tomb open, and they came near and stooped down to look in there; and they saw there a young man sitting in the midst of the tomb, fair and clothed with a robe exceedingly bright, who said to them, Wherefore are ye come? whom seek ye? Him who was crucified? He is risen and gone. But if ye believe not, stoop down and look in, and see the place where He lay, that He is not here; for He is risen and gone thither from whence He was sent. Then the women fled a frighted."

10.(b) "...leaving the tomb which they were guarding, and told all that they had seen, greatly distressed and saying, Truly He was the Son of God. Pilate answered and said, I am clean from the blood of the Son of God, but this was your pleasure. Then they all came near and besought him, and entreated him to command the centurion and the soldiers to say nothing as to the things which they had seen; for it is expedient for us (they said) to be guilty of a very great sin before God, and not to fall into the hands of the people of the Jews and be stoned. Pilate therefore commanded the centurion and the soldiers to say nothing."

12.(b) "But I Simon Peter and Andrew my brother took our nets and went to the sea; and there was with us Levi the son of Alphaeus whom the Lord." (All Quotes End)

'The Apocryphal Gospel of St. Peter' by H.B. Swete – Translator, published by Macmillan and Co. 1893

This trailing event at 12(b) likely occurred at a much later time after the Lord revealed Himself to Peter and the other disciples.

The 'Lord's Day' (weekly Sabbath) is in reference to our Lord's comments of Himself as being 'Lord of the Sabbath'. (i.e. Matthew 12:8; Mark 2:27, 28 ; Luke 6:5)

Note – The Gospel of Peter is also online at;

http://www.ccel.org/ccel/schaff/anf09.iii.ii.html

http://www.newadvent.org/fathers/1001.html

Sec. 11 The Didascalia Apostolorum Account of the Passion Event

The 'Didascalia Apostolorum' is a source document of Syriac origin written from the third century imparted later into 'The Apostolic Constitutions of the Holy Fathers' written in the fourth century where some edited descriptions are altered as prevalent.

The Translators (Editors) for the Apostolic Constituitions journal have represented the text according to a time frame of a 'civil' calendar 7 day week being Sunday through Saturday with the Passion events leading up to a Friday (Nisan 14th) crucifixion. However, that context is noticeably contradictory within the narrative body regarding a line of reference; "because thereon they crucified Me, in the midst of their festival of unleavened bread". (See Chapter xxi)

Scripture tells us (Leviticus 23:6) that the 'festival of unleavened bread within the Passover period' was recognized and observed fully by Jews between Nisan 15 to Nisan 21st regardless of whatever week days the period fell on for each changing particular year. Therefore a supposed crucifixion event occurring on Nisan 14th being the eve or opening day of Passover does not clearly equate here to: "in the midst of their festival of unleavened bread" being from Nisan 15th to Nisan 21st.

Therefore it is of my opinion, that later Editors of the fourth century would interpolate a devised time line behind the 'Apostolic Constitutions' merely to suit Constantine the Great's widespread agenda for a common 'Sun-day' unified theology.

Thus an original chronology behind the "Didascalia Apostolorum' reveals plainly the intended meanings behind the earlier evidences of truth.

* We shall emphasize here a Passover period in an earlier time when our Lord's Passion occurred on a year where Nisan 14th (full moon) fell on Thursday April 22, AD 34 with Passover being the eve to Nisan 15th which fell on a Friday as the first day of the Passover Feast; Saturday Nisan 16th as the second day; Sunday Nisan 17th as the third day; Monday Nisan 18th as the fourth day; Tuesday Nisan 19th as the fifth day; Wednesday Nisan 20th as the sixth day; and Thursday Nisan 21st being the seventh final day of the Passover feast. The meaning for the 'first day' is also evident in Leviticus 23:11 from the Greek Septuagint (LXX) Old Testament (~270 BC) that states; "and he (the priest) shall lift up the sheaf before the Lord, to be accepted for you. On the morrow (Nisan 16) of the first day (Nisan 15) the priest shall lift it up." There the 'first day' is in reference to Nisan 15th being the first day of unleavened

bread and there here should have been the narrative behind the Didascalia Apostolorum.

I have taken the liberty to quote some sections of the Didascalia Apostolorum adding the sacred calendar dates in (brackets) to clarify the Passion Narrative as it was likely intended through a Jewish reckoning of time within the Passover. It may also be reasoned here that the work of an Interpolator has added the names of some weekdays to reinforce a logic of the Passion events occurring over the course of a civil calander week.

The following text is from R. Hugh Connolly (Translator), Didascalia Apostolorum. Oxford: Clarendon Press, 1929. (Quotes Begin)

THAT IS TEACHING OF THE TWELVE HOLY APOSTLES AND DISCIPLES OF OUR SAVIOUR CHAPTER XXI

"And Judas came with the scribes and with the priests of the people, and betrayed our Lord Jesus (Yehoshua). Now this was done on the fourth day (Monday Nisan 18th) of the week (feast- period)." "For when we had eaten the passover on the third day (Sunday Nisan 17th) of the week (feast-period) at even, we went forth to the Mount of Olives; and in the night they seized our Lord Jesus (Yehoshua)." "And the next day, which was the fourth (Monday Nisan 18th) of the week (feast-period), He remained in ward in the house of Caiaphas the high priest." "...and on the same day the chiefs of the people were assembled and took counsel against Him."

"And on the next day again, which was the fifth (Tuesday Nisan 19th) of the week (feast-period), they brought Him to Pilate the governor. And He remained again in ward with Pilate the night (Wednesday Nisan 20th) after the fifth day (Tuesday Nisan 19th) of the week (feast-period)." "But when it drew on (towards day) on the Friday (Wednesday Nisan 20th), [[182]] they accused him much [Mk 15.3] before Pilate; and

91

they could show nothing that was true, but gave false witness against Him." "And they asked Him of Pilate to be put to death; and they crucified Him on the same Friday (Wednesday Nisan 20th)."

"He suffered, then, at the sixth (12:00 p.m.) hour on Friday (Wednesday)." "And these hours wherein our Lord was crucified were reckoned a day. And afterwards, again, there was darkness for three hours; and it was reckoned a night." "And again from the ninth hour (3:00 p.m.) until evening, three hours (reckoned) a day. And afterwards again, (there was) the night (Thursday Nisan 21st) of the (High) Sabbath of the Passion." "But in the Gospel of Matthew it is thus written: At even on the sabbath, when the first day of the week drew on (End the sabbaths [Nisan 15th & Nisan 21st] lighting up on one of the sabbaths = Saturday Nisan 23rd), came Mary Magdalene and the other Mary to see the tomb." "And there was a great earthquake: for an angel of the Lord came down and rolled away the stone [Mt 28.1-2]." "And again (there was) the day of the (High) Sabbath (Thursday Nisan 21st); and then three hours of the night after the Sabbath, wherein our Lord slept." "And that was fulfilled which He said: The Son of man must pass three days and three nights (Thursday Nisan 21st, Friday Nisan 22nd, Saturday Nisan 23rd) in the heart of the earth [Mt 12.40], as it is written in the Gospel." "And again it is written in David: Behold, thou hast set my days in measure [Ps 38.6 LXX]." "Now because those days and nights came short, it was so written." *Note; John 11:9 "Are there not twelve hours (of light) in a day?"

"In the night, therefore, when the first day of the week (on one of the sabbaths = Saturday Nisan 23rd) drew on, He appeared to Mary Magdalene and to Mary (See pg. 89) the daughter of James [Mt 28.1, 9 (cf. Jn 20.1, 14; Mk 16.1)]; and in the morning of the first day of the week (on one of the sabbaths-N.T. Greek) He went in to (the house of) Levi [cf. Gosp. of Peter 14]; and then He appeared also to us ourselves...."

"…But (fast) not after the custom of the former People, but according to the new testament which I have appointed you: that you may be fasting for them on the fourth day of the week (feast-period), because on the fourth (Monday Nisan 18th) of the week (feast-period) they began to destroy their souls, and apprehended Me." "For the night (Monday Nisan 18th) after the third (Sunday Nisan 17th) of the week (feast-period) belongs to the fourth (Monday Nisan 18th) of the week (feast-period), as it is written:" "There was evening and there was morning, one day [Gen 1.5]." "The evening therefore belongs to the following day: for on the third (Sunday Nisan 17th) of the week (feast-period) at even I ate My Pascha with you, and in the night (Monday Nisan 18th) they apprehended Me…."

"But fast for them also on the Friday (Wednesday Nisan 20th), because thereon they crucified Me, in the midst of their festival of unleavened bread, as it is said of old in David: In the midst of their festivals they set their signs, and they knew not.[Ps 74.4 (73.4 LXX)]…"

(Quotes End) by R. Hugh Connolly (Translator), Didascalia Apostolorum. Oxford: Clarendon Press, 1929

Here in the 'Didascalia Apostolorum' our Lord and disciples meet for unleavened bread on the end of the 'third day' (Sunday Nisan 17 of the Passover feast) and not consistent to to the evening on the 'fifth day' (understood as Thursday Nisan 13th) here the final meal is stated to have occurred in the revised work over of the 'Apostolic Constitutions'. Thus being a ritual here along with the Gospel's 'first day of unleavened bread' that made our Lord's feast meals last for a total of 3 settings only.

Here the arrest of our Lord would have occurred a short time later on the 'fourth day' being the nightly beginning of Monday Nisan 18th.

Also, where the sixth day is stated in the Didascalia Apostolorum and interpreted as a Friday on the civil calendar week, the sixth day may be reasoned in the order of feast days as occurring on Wednesday Nisan 20th of our Lord's Passion.

The interpretation behind this transcript is remedied from the Greek New Testament where 'one of the sabbaths' (mia ton sabbaton) is translated directly from within the Gospel's resurrection verses.

* Through the past centuries these writings were probably re-edited and interpolated by Gentile scholars where the original intended Jewish meanings were dropped and changed to non-Jewish meanings becoming less properly understood, and over-looked repeatedly through later times. See the Didascalia Apostolorum online at;

http://www.bombaxo.com/didascalia.html

Sec. 12 Joseph of Arimathaea's Passion Account

* 'The Gospel of Nicodemus' is taken from a section of a book known as the 'Acts of Pilate' (Pilate's account of the Passion Event to the Emperor Tiberius Caeser) portraying a scene where various Galilean bystanders witness a transfiguration moment of the post-resurrected Yehoshua being beside his disciples on Mount Mamilch. The news of this incident spreads quickly to the high priests back in Jerusalem who issue a search party for the missing Yehoshua. Joseph from Arimathaea who was

imprisoned and later separated (in seclusion at home for 40 days from the resurrection day on Saturday Nisan 23rd) is then discovered by officials and returned to Jerusalem for conciliatory means through Nicodemus with an examination by council members.

* I have taken the liberty to supplement sacred calendar dates in (brackets) to clarify the account's narrative.

Here we have GESTA PILATI (Acts of Pilate)

By W. 0. CLOUGH. B. A. (Translator) INDIANAPOLIS, ROBERT DOUGLASS. 1880

THE ACTS OF PILATE Chapters 15 -16 (Sec.199 – 202)

(Quotes Begin)

"Blessed [be] the Lord God, who hath delivered Israel from shedding innocent blood; and blessed [be] God, who sent his angel, and covered me under his wings. And he kissed them, and set a table for them; and they ate and drank, and slept there."

"And they rose (Thursday Sivan 4th) in the morning; and Joseph (after 40 days of seclusion) saddled his ass, and traveled (secular day) with them, and they came into the holy city Jerusalem. And there met them all the people, crying out, and saying: Peace [be] in thy coming in, father Joseph! To whom he answered and said: The peace of the Lord [be] upon all the people! And they all kissed him. And they prayed with Joseph, and were terrified at the sight of him."

"And Nicodemus took him into his house, and made a great feast (peace token banquet), and called Annas and Caiaphas, and the elders and chief priests and Levites, to his house. And making merry, and eating and drinking with Joseph, they blessed God, and went every one to his own house. And Joseph remained in the house of Nicodemus."

"And on the next day (Friday Sivan 5th), which is the preparation, the priests and the rulers of the synagogue and the Levites rose early, and came to the house of Nicodemus. And Nicodemus met them, and said to them: Peace to you! And they said to him: Peace to thee and Joseph, and to thy house and Joseph's house! And Nicodemus brought them into his house."

"And the counsel sat; and Joseph sat between Annas and Caiaphas, and no one dared to say a word. And Joseph said to them: Why have you called me? And they made signs with their eyes to Nicodemus that he should speak with Joseph."

"And Nicodemus opening his mouth, said: Father Joseph, thou knowest that the reverend teachers, priests, and Levites seek to hear a word from thee. And Joseph said: Ask?"

"And Annas and Caiaphas, taking up the law, adjured Joseph saying: Give glory to the God of Israel, and give confession to him, that thou wilt not hide any word from us."

"And they said to him: With grief were we grieved that thou didst beg the body of Jesus (Yehoshua), and wrap it in clean linen, and lay it in a tomb."

"Therefore we shut thee up in a house where there was no window, and put a lock and a seal on the gate; and on the first day of the week (one of the [integral] sabbaths = Saturday Nisan 23rd) we opened the gates, and found thee not."

"We were therefore exceedingly grieved, and astonishment came over all the people of God. And therefore hast thou been sent for; and now tell us what has happened."

"Then said Joseph: On the day of the preparation (Friday Nisan 22nd), about the tenth hour (4 p.m.), you shut me in, and I remained there the whole Sabbath (Saturday Nisan 23rd) in full. And when midnight (possibly at 'even' in the 12th hour before 6 p.m.) came, as I was standing and praying, the house where you shut me in was hung up by the four corners, and there was a flashing of light in mine eyes. And I fell to the ground trembling."

"Then some one lifted me up from the place where I had fallen, and poured over me an abundance of water from the head even to the feet, and put round my nostrils the odor of a wonderful ointment, and rubbed my face with the water itself, as if washing me, and kissed me, and said to me, Joseph, fear not; but open thine eyes, and see who it is that speaks to thee. And looking, I saw Jesus (Yehoshua); and being terrified, I thought it was a phantom. And with prayer and the commandments I spoke to him, and he spoke with me."

"And I said to him: Art thou Babbi Elias ? And he said to me: I am not Elias. And I said: Who art thou, my lord? And he said to me:"

"I am Jesus (Yehoshua), whose body thou didst beg from Pilate, and wrap in clean linen; and thou didst lay a napkin on my face, and didst lay me in thy new tomb, and roll a stone to the door of the tomb."

"Then I said to him that was speaking to me: Show me, Lord, where I laid thee. And he led me, and showed me the place where I laid him, and the linen which I had put on him, and the napkin which I had wrapped upon his face; and I knew that it was Jesus (Yehoshua). And he took hold of me with his hand, and put me in the midst of my house though the gates were shut, and put me in my bed, and said to me : Peace to thee ! And he kissed me, and said to me : For forty days (Saturday Nisan 23 – Wednesday Sivan 3) go not out of thy house ; for, lo, I go to my brethren into Galilee."

(Quotes continue...)

"Chapter 16 — And the rulers of the synagogue, and the priests and the Levites, hearing these words from Joseph, became as if were dead, and fell to the ground, and fasted until the ninth hour (e.g. 3 p.m.). And Joseph and Nicodemus entreated them, saying:

Arise and stand upon your feet, and taste bread, and comfort your souls, seeing that tomorrow (Saturday Sivan 6th) is the (Pentecost) Sabbath of the Lord. And they arose, and entreated the Lord, and ate and drank, and went every man to his own house.

And on the (Pentecost) sabbath (Saturday Sivan 6th) the teachers and doctors sat questioning each other, and saying: what is this wrath that has come upon us?" (All Quotes End)

Compare to Acts 2:6, 12.

6. "Now when this was noised abroad, the multitude that came together, and were confounded, because that every man heard them speak in his own language."

12. "And they were all amazed, and were in doubt, saying one to another, What meaneth this?"

* The possible hidden scenes reasoned behind here consisted of a rash burial with a quickly found one piece cloth garment (Mth 27:59 ; Mrk 14:51, 52) placed around Yehoshua's body on Wednesday Nisan 20th a feast preparation (secular) day. After the feast high sabbath (Jhn 19:31) of Thursday Nisan 21st passed, Joseph (likely with Pilate's permission influenced through Nicodemus' Sanhedrin Council status) returns to the tomb on the preparation (secular) day of Friday Nisan 22nd with purchased fine linen (Mrk 15:46) to be made into strips and wraps the body with prepared myrrh (Jhn 19:39) under a guarded watch prior (Luk 23:56) to the weekly Sabbath. Thus the body would have decayed for about a day and a half until the customary burial and not beyond the full three days and three nights margin.

The linen strips and headdress (Jhn 20:6, 7) are re-discovered neatly rolled up on the evening (end) of Saturday Nisan 23rd when Peter comes to the sepulcher. The guards quickly bring word to the priests who seek for Joseph (who was placed a day earlier in the holding cell) knowing that he was the last person working in the tomb but he is not revealed until 40 days later.

* Note here when calculating the testimonial chronological details in reference to the belief of a traditional Passion time line. There the confusion of wrath amongst rulers would have occurred on Sunday Iyyar 29th, not matching the Sabbath day which Joseph reveals being a Sabbath on Sivan 6 being 43 days from the Sabbath resurrection.

*The sign of Jonah also leaves little merit when the missing Joseph was with the raised Yehoshua at an evening time on the weekly sabbath before a traditional Sunday morning resurrection. etc> Luke 24:4 "And it came to pass, as they were much perplexed thereabout, behold, two men (Yehoshua & Joseph) stood by them in shining garments."

See – The Gospel of Nicodemus with Joseph's account of a resurrection experience with the risen Lord on line at;

http://www.ccel.org/ccel/schaff/anf08.vii.xii.xvi.html

Sec. 13 The Greek Syntax of Grammar

The Biblical resurrection verses for those that display (mia ton sabbaton = one of sabbaths) is shown as a partitive genitive case function where one sabbath is identified in association to a larger group of sabbaths between the Passover 'First Fruits' offering leading up to Pentecost.

(i.e.) 'μιαν σαββατων' (Koine Greek) as 'one of [the] sabbaths' in the second segment of Mth 28:1 or 'μια των σαββατων' as 'one of [the] sabbaths' in Mrk 16:2 ; Luk 24:1 ; Jhn 20:1 ; Act 20:7, and I Cor 16:2.

See also; http://www.bcbsr.com/greek/gcase.html

(Quote Begins) "Partitive (Wholative) Genitive [which is a part of]" "The substantive in the genitive denotes the whole of which the head noun is a part. This is a phenomenological use of the genitive that requires the head noun to have a lexical nuance indicating portion. For example, "some of the Pharisees," "one of you," "a tenth of the city," "the branch of the tree," "a piece of pie." "Luke 19:8 half of my possessions" "Rom 11:17 some of the branches" (Quotes End)

* Here are quotes from a book named; Ancient Greek – A New Approach by Carl A.P. Ruck, The Massachusetts Institute of Technology Press 1996 Pg 42 (Quotes Begin)

"In the ablatival function, the genitive often indicates the totality from which a part is separated. The meaning is the so-called partitive genitive."

"The ablatival function of the genitive is often clarified by the use of specific prepositions (or separable prefixes) that design separation." (Quotes End)

However, the first and second segments of Matthew 28:1 as a 2 fold expression is simply compounded together where the plurality of the contrasting 'sabbaths' appear interwoven but in a duality hold separate explicable binary meanings.

In Matthew 28:1 the first segment as 'οωέ δέ σαββάτων' is stating that the two annual Passover high sabbaths (genitive of separation) had already passed.

There 'οωέ σαββατων' as 'Late (adverb) moreover sabbaths' in Matthew 28:1 is stating that the 2 High sabbaths (Nisan 15 & 21) of the Passover period had completed, thus expressing a similar context in time comparable to Verse 12 in the Gospel of St. Peter (Quotes Begin).

"Now it was the last day of unleavened bread, and many went out of the city returning to their houses, the feast (Nisan 15-21) being at an end. And we the twelve disciples of the Lord wept and were in sorrow, and every man withdrew to his house sorrowing for what had come to pass." (Quotes End)

The Apocryphal Gospel of St. Peter – H.B. Swete

* In the second segment of Matthew 28:1 we see 'μίαν σαββάτων' that is showing 'one' sabbath (Nisan 23) as an integral (partitive – genitive) day in association to a larger group of similar weekly sabbaths.

* All N.T. verses (e.g. Mrk 16:2; Luk 24:1; Jhn 20:1, 19; Act 20:7; and 1 Cor 16:2) with the consistent uniform phrase 'μια των σαββατων' is interpreted as 'one of sabbaths' with NO prepositions nor with any inflection upon them. There the phrase 'μια των σαββατων' stands up unmodified where the direct meaning is in relation to the group of seven weekly Sabbaths between Passover and Pentecost that is clearly referenced in Leviticus 23:15. Hence, Yehoshua must have resurrected on one of those seven Sabbaths and not to be understood presumably on the first day (Sunday) of the week as was mandated and regulated in the fourth century by Constantine's personal pagan antics.

Sec. 14 Various Renditions of the St. Matthew 28:1 Resurrection
      Passage

(All Quotations Begin)

St. Jerome's Latin Vulgate AD 382

"vespere autem sabbati quae lucescit in priman sabbati venit Maria
Magdalena et altera Maria videre sepulchrum"

Jon Wiclif 1380

"But in the euentide of the saboth that bigynneth to schyne in the first
dai of the wike: marie mawdeleyn cam an other marie to see the
sepulcre."

William Tyndale 1526

"The Sabboth daye at even which dauneth the morowe after the
Sabboth Mary Magdalene and the other Mary came to se the sepulcre."

Myles Coverdale New Testament 1535

"Upon the euenynge of the Sabbath holy daye, which dawneth ye
morow of the first daye of ye Sabbathes, came Mary Magdalene and ye
other Mary, to se ye sepulcre."

Jean Calvin's Commentary 1536

"Now in the evening of the Sabbaths, which began to dawn towards the first of the Sabbaths, came Mary Magdalene, and the other Mary, to see the sepulcher."

Thomas Cranmer (Great Bible) 1539

"VPON an euening of the Sabbothes, which dawneth the first daye of the Sabbathes, came Mary Magdalene and the other Mary, to se the sepulcre."

The Geneva Bible 1557

"ABOUT the later ende of the Sabbath day, when the first day of the weeke began to dawne, Mary Magdalne, and the other Marie came to see the sepulcher."

The Bishop's Bible 1568

"In the later ende of the Sabboth day, whiche dawneth the first daye of the weke, came Marie Magdalen, and the other Marie, to see the sepulchre."

Doway Reimms 1582

"AND in the euening of the Sabboth vvhich davvneth on the first of the Sabboth, came Marie Magdalene, and the other Marie to see the sepulcher."

Authorised King James (KJV) 1611

"In the end of the Sabbath, as it began to dawne towards the first day of the weeke, came Mary Magdalene, and the other Mary, to see the sepulcher."

Young's Literal Translation (YLT) 1862

"And on the eve of the sabbaths, at the dawn, toward the first of the sabbaths, came Mary the Magdalene, and the other Mary, to see the sepulchre."

Julia E. Smith Translation 1876 (First Women Translator)

"AND after the Sabbaths, in the shining forth to one of the Sabbaths, came Mary Magdalene and the other Mary to behold the tomb."

The Revised (King James) Version (RV) 1881

"Now late on the sabbath day, as it began to dawn toward the first day of the week, came Mary Magdalene and the other Mary to see the sepulchre."

TRANSLATION OF THE NEW TESTAMENT FROM THE ORIGINAL GREEK

REV. W.B. GODBEY 1901

"And late on the Sabbath-day, on the dawn toward the first of the Sabbaths, Mary Magdalene and the other Mary came to see the sepulcher."

Adolphus S. Worrell New Testament 1904

"Now, in the end of Sabbaths, at the dawning toward the first day of the Sabbaths, came Mary Magdalene and the other Mary to see the sepulcher."

The Sacred Scriptures / Concordant Literal New Testament (CLNT) A.E. Knoch 1927

"Now it is the evening of the sabbaths. At the lighting up into one of the sabbaths came Mary Magdalene and the other Mary to behold the sepulcher."

The Kingdom Interlinear (The Watchtower Society) (TKI) 1969

"After but of sabbaths, to the [day] lighting up into one of sabbaths, came Mary the Magdalene and the other Mary to view the tomb."

Jay P. Green Sr. Interlinear Bible (TIB) 1976

"After the sabbaths, at the dawning into the first of the sabbaths, Mary Magdalene and the other Mary came to the grave."

NOUUM TESTAMENTUM LATINE – CURANTE HENRICO I. WHITE 1911

"Uespere autem sabbati, quae lucescit in prima sabbati, uenit Maria Magdalene, et altera Maria uidere sepulchrum."

GREEK TEXT – STEPHENS 1550 – TEXTUS RECEPTUS

"οψε δε σαββατων τη επιφωσκουση εις μιαν σαββατων ηλθεν μαρια η μαγδαληνη και η αλλη μαρια θεωρησαι τον ταφον"

GREEK TEXT – WESCOTT & HORT 1885 – CODEX SINAITICUS

"οψε δε σαββατων, τη επιφωσκούση εις μίαν σαββάτων, ηλθεν Μαρία η Μαγδαληνη και η αλλη Μαρία θεωρησαι τον τάφον."

See Online Greek Renderings;

The Transliterated Greek Text (The Online Bible Data Base) "opse de sabbatôn tê epiphôskousê eis mian sabbatôn êlthen a=mariam tsb=maria ê magdalênê kai ê allê maria theôrêsai ton taphon."

http://bibledbdata.org/onlinebibles/greek_translit/40_028.html

The Interlinear NRSV-NIV Parallel New Testament In Greek and English by Alfred Marshall 1991 Zondervan Publishers.

"But late of (the) sabbaths, at the drawing on toward one of (the) sabbaths, came Mary the Magdelene and the other Mary to view the grave." See Online (Page 98);

http://books.google.ca/books?id=VhWFUvB5wDUC&printsec=frontcove ramp;source=gbs_atb#v=onepage&q&f=false

HALLELUYAH SCRIPTURES – C.J. KOSTER 1993

"Now after the Shabbath, toward dawn on one of the Shabbathoth, Miryam from Magdala and the other Miryam came to see the tomb."

http://www.HalleluYahScriptures.com

Word Study Greek-English New Testament – Paul R. McReynolds 1999

"Evening but of sabbaths in the dawning on in one of sabbaths went Mariam the Magdalene and the other Maria to watch the tomb."

See online (Pg. 117);
http://books.google.ca/books?id=zfOUXPcJ71MC&pg=PR7&dq=The+Int erlinear+Greek-English+New+Testament&hl=en#v=onepage&q=The%20Interlinear%20 GreekEnglish%20New%20Testament&f=false

Scripture 4 All 2005

"Evening YET OF-SABBATHS to-THE ON-LIGHTING INTO ONE OF SABBATHS CAME MARY THE MAGDALENE AND THE OTHER MARY TO-behold THE sepulcher." See Online;

http://www.scripture4all.org/OnlineInterlinear/NTpdf/

(All Quotations End)

My literal English – KOINE GREEK interlinear;

"Late (οψε) except (δε) sabbaths (σαββατων) to the (τη) lighting-up (επιφωσκουση) into (εις) one of (μιαν) sabbaths (σαββατων) Mary (μαρια) Magdalene (μαγδαληνη) and (και) the (η) other (αλλη) Mary (μαρια) observed (θεωρησαι) the (τον) sepulcher (ταφον)."

My literal Interpretation of Matthew 28:1;

"Late (adverb) (post-after-end) more-over (the annual Passover) sabbaths, (plural) [genitive of separation] as it was lighting up (twi-lighting or the torch lighting period) on one(a cardinal number) of the [a partitive genitive case function] sabbaths (plural) came Mary Magdalene and the other Mary to view the tomb."

Please Note – The other Gospel resurrection passages of Mark 16:2, Luke 24:1, and John 20:1 are shown with 'μια των σαββατων' (a partitive genitive case function) in the Koine Greek being transliterated as 'mia ton sabbaton' and translated directly into English as on 'one of the sabbaths'.

Sec. 15 The Actual Resurrection Phrase

Although the phrase 'mia ton sabbatwn' may be synonymous in meaning with the 'first day of the week' scripturally it is not duly supported. The phrase 'first (ordinal) day of the week' could have appeared as; 'πρώτο ημέρα του εβδομάδας' i.e. 'first (πρώτο) day (ημέρα) of the (του) week (εβδομάδας)' and transliterated as 'prote hemera tis hebdomata' in the original Koine Greek verses of; Matthew 28:1, Mark 16:2, Luke 24:1, St. John 20:1,19; Acts 20:7, and 1 Corinthians 16:2 in the New Testament but does NOT appear anywhere in any way, shape or form.

The word 'εβδομάδας' in the Koine Greek for 'week' does appear respectively in certain aspects of the Septuagint LXX Old Testament (~ 270 B.C.) i.e. Ex 34:22; Lev 23:15, 16, 25; Num 28:26; Deut 16:9, 10, 16; II Cron 8:13, and Dan 9:24,25, 26, 27; 10:2, 3.

Secondly, the phrase 'the first (ordinal) of the sabbaths' could have appeared as 'της πρωτον των σαββάτων' i.e. 'the (της) first (πρωτον) of (των) sabbaths (σαββάτων)' in the original Koine Greek for the resurrection verses but does not for the most part. However, 'πρωτη ημερα των αζυμων' i.e. 'first (πρωτη) day (ημερα) of the (των) unleaveneds (αζυμων)' = 'first (ordinal) day of unleaved (bread)' is translated accurately for Mark 14:12 along with the most part of Matthew 26:17 and Luke 22:7.

The verse of Mark 16:9 in the original Greek is shown as 'πρώτη σάββατου' transliterated as 'protos sabbatou' which is translated literally to mean 'first (ordinal) sabbath (singular)'. Here the long ending of Mark 16:9–20 is critically regarded as an extension interpolated at a later time and does not exist in the earlier and older manuscripts. The Codex Alexandrinus, Codex Sinaiticus, Sinaitic Syriac, Armenian and oldest Georgian manuscripts show no support for the long ending of St. Mark 16:9-20.

** Here is A.E. Knoch's Concordant (literal) Version 'The Sacred Scriptures' (1927) Concordant Publishing Concern 2823 EAST SIXTH STREET LOS ANGELES,

CAL, U.S.A. (Bible Quotes Begin)

Matthew 28:1

"Now it is the evening of the sabbaths. At the lighting up into one of the sabbaths came Mary Magdalene and the other Mary to behold the sepulcher."

Mark 16:2

"And, very early in the morning on one of the sabbaths, they are coming to the tomb at the rising of the sun."

Luke 24:1

"Now in the early depths of one of the sabbaths, they, and certain others together with them, came to the tomb, bringing the spices which they make ready."

John 20:1

"Now, on one of the sabbaths, Miriam Magdalene is coming to the tomb in the morning, there being still darkness, and is observing the stone taken away from the door of the tomb."

John 20:18

"It being, then, the evening of that day, one of the sabbaths, and the doors having been locked where the disciples were gathered together, because of fear of the Jews, Jesus (Yehoshua) came and stood in the midst and is saying to them, "Peace to you!"

Acts 20:7

"Now on one of the sabbaths, at our having gathered to break bread, Paul argued with them, being about to be off on the morrow. Besides, he prolonged the word unto midnight."

1 Corinthians 16:2

"On one of the sabbaths let each of you lay aside by himself in store that in which he should be prospered, that no collections may be occurring then, whenever I may come." (Bible Quotes End)

Here are some further quotes from A.E. Knoch's 'Concordant Commentary' (1968); Concordant Publishing Concern 15570 Knochaven Road, Santa Clarita, CA 91350, U.S.A. (Quotes Begin)

Matthew 28:1

"One of the sabbaths" is the only correct translation of the phrase usually rendered "the first day of the week". The word first is not there. It is simply one, and is applied to the eleventh hour (Mt.20:12), which, in that case, was last, not first. The word day is not in the text at all. The word "week" is in the plural, and is precisely the same as the form in the preceding sentence. If it is rendered "sabbaths" there it must also be "sabbaths" here. So, there is no recourse but to translate "one of the sabbaths."

"The key to this expression lies in the law of the Firstfruits (Lev.23:9-14). Ending with the day before Pentecost there were seven sabbaths (Lev.23:15) from the day with the waving of the "sheaf". These are referred to in the phrase "one of the sabbaths". Every mention of this phrase places it between the Passover and Pentecost, (1Co.16:2 and Acts 20:1 and 6). And the other occurrences refer to our Lord's resurrection (Mk.16:2; Lu.24:1; Jn.20:1-19). He was raised on a sabbath, not the first day of the week, which would be our Sunday."

"His resurrection on the Sabbath is a token that His work was complete. Redemption is now a matter of entering into His stopping, not the beginning of a new week of toil and labor." (Pg. 55-6) (Quotes End)

See; http://www.concordant.org/version/CLNT_Intro.htm

* However, some of Knoch's interpretation on the resurrection timing (closely suited to AD 34) is limited in my opinion.There the 'sign of Jonah' (Mth 12:39,40) of a 3 days and 3 nights time line falls short under

Knoch's Passion time frame. His chronology is based strongly on his biblical reasoning of scripture for a Passover Thursday (Nisan 14th) crucifixion and a Saturday evening (Nisan 16th) resurrection. There he believed that the resurrection occurred on a Saturday Nisan 16th signifying our Lord being presented as a first fruit offering to our heavenly Father on the Hebrew first fruits sheaf offering day. In his time frame also there is no secular day available between the two separated sabbaths (i.e. compare; Mrk 16:1, Luk 23:56) for the purchase of spices and burial preparations of Yehoshua.

In the N.T. resurrection verses of Matthew 28:1; Mark 16:2; Luke 24:1; and St. John 20:1,19 of the New Testament we commonly find the Koine Greek phrases; 'μιαν σαββατων' transliterated as 'mian sabbaton' or 'μια των σαββατων' transliterated as 'mia ton sabbaton' and translated to literally mean; 'one (cardinal) of (the) sabbaths As well other close words to this phrase can be found similarly within other N.T. verses such as; Acts 20:7, 1 Corinthians 16:2 and Colossians 2:16.

If the resurrection verses were to have been understood in an ordinal sense the Koine word; 'πρώτη' trans-literated as 'protos' for 'first' could have easily been used but does not occur regularly in the passages of interest regarding such matters.

The translators through the subsequent centuries may have commonly based their Passion narrative from an illusory premise established by the enforced regimes of Constantine the Great. Therefore, a breakdown in scriptural dissimulation likely replaced the original Greek resurrection verses where 'μιαν σαββατων' depicts a much broader sense in a Hebrew understanding for those who are able to understand it in the proper context as was initially intended.

The Biblical resurrection verses for those that display (mia ton sabbaton = one of sabbaths) is represented as a partitive genitive case function where one (1) sabbath is recognized in association to a similar group or a week of (7) sabbaths (i.e. Lev 23:15).

The Koine Greek word 'μια' transliterated as 'mia' and translated as 'one' (cardinal) is found in the Greek Septuagint (~250 BC) O.T. references such as; Deuteronomy 12:14 (one of the tribes), 15:7 ; 19:5,11 (one of the cities), Joshua 10:2 (one of the chief cities), Ruth 2:13 (one of thy servants), 1 Kings 2:36 (one of the priests), and 2 Kings 15:2 (one of the tribes).

Outside the resurrection verses the Koine Greek word 'μια' is found in other N.T. references such as; Matthew 5:19 (one of the commandments), 26:69 (one servant girl); Mark 14:66 (one of the maids), and Luke 5:12 (one of the cities), 5:17 (one of the days), 13:10 (one of the synagogues), 17:22, 20:1. (one of the days) and Acts 21:7 (one day).

Outside the resurrection verses the Koine Greek word 'σαββατων' transliterated as 'sabbaton' and translated as 'sabbaths' can be found in Luke 4:16 and Acts 13:14, 16:13 (day of the sabbaths). Each example exhibits a partitive genitive case function where one of something is displayed as a fractional margin in association or possession to a larger group in a mass resemblance of the same thing.

As well we have numerous Koine Greek Septuagint Old Testament verses where the words 'μια' as 'one', 'ημέρα' as 'day', or 'πρώτη' as 'first' appears in various combined segments. These may be observed at; Genesis 27:45, 33:13, Leviticus 22:28, 23:35,39,40., Numbers 11:19, Deuteronomy 16:4, Judges 20:23, 1 Kings 2:34, 27:1, 3 Kings 4:22, Ezra 3:6, 10:13,16,17., Ester 3:13, 8:12, Nehemiah 8:2,18, Isaiah 9:14, 66:8, Daniel 10:12, and Zacharius 14:7.

In the N.T. we have a few examples shown in Mark 14:12, Acts 20:17, and Phillipians 1:5. There the various examples are usually two words combined togeather where 'μια ημέρα' is commonly translated as 'one day' and 'ημέρα μια' as 'day one' but mis- interpreted as the 'first day' along with 'πρώτη ημέρα' more precisely. The segment 'μια ημέρα' as 'one day' may be regarded in a fractional sense for a position of tense within time. Again for the resurrection verse of St. Matthew 28:1 the words 'μιαν σαββατων' is rationalized as 'one of sabbaths' being one sabbath within a group of seven weekly sabbaths. (e.g. Lev 23:15)

Sec. 16   Re-Analysis of Matthew 28:1

* In light of;

'A GRAMMAR OF THE GREEK NEW TESTAMENT IN THE LIGHT OF HISTORICAL RESEARCH'

Af T.' ROBERTSON, M.A., D.D., LL.D Pg. 646

(Quotes Begin)

"Hence in Mt. 28: 1 οψε σαββατων may be either late on the Sabbath or after the Sabbath. Either has good support Moulton^ is uncertain, while Blass (2) prefers 'after.' It is a point for exegesis, not for grammar, to decide. If Matthew has in mind just before sunset, 'late on' would be his idea; if he means after sunset, then 'after' is correct."

(Quotes End)

A GRAMMAR OF THE GREEK NEW TESTAMENT IN THE LIGHT OF HISTORICAL RESEARCH

HODDER & STOUGHTON NEW YORK GEORGE H. DORAN COMPANY COPYRIGHT, 1914 BY GEORGE H. DORAN COMPANY

The Greek word 'οψε' in Matthew 28:1 is shown as 'end' in the Authorised 1611 KJV and as 'late' (of the sabbath) in the Revised 1881 KJV edition .

The New Scofield Reference Edition KJV study bible by the Oxford University Press, 1967 shows a footnote for St. Matthew 28:1 (Quote Begins)

"the text should read, 'the end of sabbaths'". (Quote Ends)

http://www.biblestudytools.com/commentaries/scofield-reference-notes/matthew/matthew-28.html

*For the intermediate segment of Matthew 28:1 we shall elaborate further on the partitive genitive phrase 'μιαν σαββατων'. In a traditional sense this phrase has been thought to mean 'the first day of the week'. There the Greek word 'μιαν' for 'one of' being feminine in gender and cardinal in meaning has been grammatically mistranslated to an ordinal word as 'first'. The Greek word 'ημέρα' for 'day' does not literally exist anywhere in the original texts but has been added in the translated resurrection verses anyhow. The Greek word 'σαββατων' literally as 'sabbaths' has been interpreted and thought to mean 'week'. Therefore all passages for 'the first day of the week' are grammatically transformed as a foreign phrase implying a secondary meaning incomparable to the original content as initially intended by the Greek written Jewish authors.

An Expository Dictionary of New Testament Words by

W.E. Vine shows the word 'one' as a numeral reference, (Quote Begins) "in the phrase 'the first day of the week,' lit. and idiomatically, 'one of sabbaths'..." (Quote Ends) pg. 446 by Thomas Nelson Publishers 4th printing in 1983. See 1520 (5) under alphabetical 'O' for 'one' on line;

http://www2.mf.no/bibelprog/vines?word=

* In, 'THE ANALYTICAL GREEK LEXICON' published

by SAMUEL BAGSTER and SONS 1870 and later in 1970 (DEC. 6th printing) by the ZONDERVAN PUBLISHING HOUSE thus shows; (Quotes Begin)

TABLES OF PARADIGMS of GREEK DE-CLENSIONS AND CONJUGATIONS with EXPLANATORY GRAMMATICAL REMARKS

Pg. i (4) (Quote Begins)

"The gen. pl. [genitive plural], in all genders, ends in ωv. This is the case also in every declension without exception." (Quotes End)

http://www.archive.org/stream/AnalyticalGreekLexiconAlphabeticalInfl exionGreekNtScriptures.Bagsters/AnalyticalGreekLexicon.Bagsters.1870 .#page/n23/mode/2up

* Thus all of the Koine Greek N.T. resurrection passages (i.e. Mth 28:1 ; Mrk 16:2 ; Luk 24:1 ; Jhn 20:1 ; Act 20:7) show the phrase 'μια των σαββατων' literally in meaning as on 'one of the sabbaths' where the pronoun 'one' is a part division of the plural noun showing 'sabbaths'.

The traditional translators also differentiate to identify the Greek word 'σαββατων' in the first and second segments of Matthew 28:1 where 'σαββατων' appears twice in the same passage being plural in meaning at both instances. There instead, they have revised a dual meaning for the word 'σαββατων' to mis-translate it as 'sabbath' or as 'week' other

116

then 'sabbaths' where it is plural at both instances when rendered correctly into the proper English.

* Note – Where 'σαββατων' has been mistranslated to mean 'sabbath' (singular) in the first segment of Matthew 28:1 the word 'οψε' as 'late' becomes a misconstrued reference to the time within a (single) day by itself.

Elsewhere the traditionalists have mistranslated the word 'week' to fit all other resurrection verses where the original Greek word 'σαββατων' = 'sabbaton' =' sabbaths' was given.

* Note – The phrase the 'first day of the week' could have appeared as; 'πρώτο ημέρα του εβδομάδας' e.g. 'first (πρώτο) day (ημέρα) of the (του) week (εβδομάδας)' in the original Greek N.T. Texts for the verses of; Matthew 28:1, Mark 16:2, Luke 24:1, St. John 20:1,19; Acts 20:7, and 1 Corinthians 16:2 in the New Testament but does NOT appear anywhere in any way, shape or form.

However, 'πρωτη ημερα των αζυμων' = 'first (ordinal) day of unleavened (bread)' is translated fairly accurate for Mark 14:12 showing that the phrase 'first day' has been interpreted correctly like other N.T. passages such as Matthew 26:17 and Luke 22:7.

It appears that the traditionalists state their interpretation of the resurrection passages (apart from Semitic influences) to form their translation based merely on Constantine's fourth century mandate yet contrary to God's earlier written word.

* Note – (Quote Begins) 'Philology' (is) "the study of written records, their authenticity in original form, and the determination of their meaning." (Quote Ends) The Random House Dictionary

* Note – (Quote Begins) An 'anachronism' (is) "an event that is chronologically out of place, especially one appropriate to an earlier period." (Quote Ends) The Random House Dictionary

Sec. 17 Three Separate Interpretations of Matthew 28:1

Traditional Bible Scholars who believe in a Sunday morning resurrection understand 'Matthew 28:1' as a key resurrection passage which determines the chronology behind all other resurrection verses as stated elsewhere in the New Testament.

 In the opening segment of Matthew 28:1 the Koine Greek word 'οωέ' transliterated as 'opse' may be understood like a preposition that modifies the remainder of the sentence.

 Thus 'οωέ' is interpreted as 'late' being an 'adverb' in a post sense where it has an effect to mean 'after' or at the 'end' of the sabbath(s) where 2 sabbaths (annual & weekly) coincided simultaneously (Saturday Nisan 15th) together on the exact same day. There the Greek word 'σαββατων' = 'sabbaton' = 'sabbaths' has been theologically interpreted and simplified to a singular meaning at 'the end of the sabbath' (KJV) commonly considered to be the beginning (Sunday Nisan 16th) 'on the first day of the week'. The sense here is being that the 'first day' was ablative from the sabbath(s) day.

Also the phrase 'one of the sabbaths' has an idiomatic understanding that proportions Civil calendar weekdays in a numerical order from weekly sabbath to weekly sabbath. Thus 'one of the sabbaths' has been reasoned in an idiomatic sense as equal to 'the first day of the week'.

Therefore, it is also reasoned that Yehoshua rose as a 'first fruit' (St. Jhn 20:17) on 'the first day of the week' simultaneous in timing to the 'first fruits' (Lev 23:10, 11) being offered up by the high temple priests on Sunday Nisan 16 being the second day of Passover.

* Consider as well a Sabbatarian synopsis to those who believe in a Sabbath day resurrection with a distinct understanding where the word 'οωέ' (Mth 28:1) may be interpreted as 'later' being an 'adjective' where it has a sense to mean 'near the end' or 'just before the closing' of the sabbaths where 2 sabbaths coincided separately on different days (Thursday Nisan 15th & Saturday Nisan 17th) within the same civil calendar week. The emphasis lies 'later' on Saturday Nisan 17 as the weekly sabbath (in the genitive) being the 'first of sabbaths' (YLT) in the resurrection passages and 'πρώτη σάββατου' for the 'first sabbath' (Mrk 16:2) of seven weekly sabbaths (Lev 23:15) on the sacred calendar after a Friday Nissan 16 sheaf offering day as; Nisan 17, Nisan 24, Iyyar 1, Iyyar 8, Iyyar 15, Iyyar 22, and Iyyar 29 to Pentecost on Friday Sivan 6th.

Many Others, divert partially in this chronological scale with Pentecost arriving instead on a Sunday Sivan 8th after the 50 day count commences on Sunday Nisan 18 interpreted as the sheaf offering day after the weekly Nisan 17 Sabbath.

Thus, in the first segment of Matthew 28:1 we have various takes for 'οψε' on the resurrection moment being positioned together by the reciprocation of grammar and theology alike.

119

Thus 'οψε' equals; (i) 'later' as an adjective in time 'near or before the end' of the sabbaths. (ii) 'late' as a pronoun in time as related to the sabbaths now ended, finished and completed. (iii) 'late' as an adverb in time as 'beyond, post, and after' the 'sabbaths'. The term 'late' from 'οψε' also forms here a genitive clause of separation in relation to the head-noun 'σαββατων' being shown as 'sabbaths' when understood correctly.

* Here as well, a continued all in depth analysis shall reveal a post Passover-feast resurrection event on a weekly Sabbath day as revealed in Matthew 28:1.

'Late' (adverb) (genitive of separation) [After] the [Passover high] sabbaths 'οωέ σαββατων' (Friday Nisan 15th + Thursday Nisan 21st) on 'one of sabbaths' (CLNT) from 'μιαν σαββατων' being (Saturday Nisan 23rd) (partitive genitive) as one of the seven integral sabbaths (between Passover & Pentecost)...etc.

This describes and combines all of the 'special sabbaths' as they were laid out consecutively within the Jewish sacred calendar and has little reflection on the civic calendar 'week' (an added word that is entirely omitted in the original Greek form). This group of seven weekly sabbaths for the Hebrew 3794th year (since creation) shoud have been; Nisan 23, Nisan 30, Iyyar 7, Iyyar 14, Iyyar 21, Iyyar 28, and Sivan 6th. Here likely, Yehoshua resurrected on the 1rst weekly sabbath of a group of 7 sabbaths (i.e. Lev 23:15) in reference to the sacred calendar being Matthew's intention recalling the passion story in a logical narrative of time sequence.

The significance underlies here in the enigmatic transliterated phrases 'mian sabbaton' or 'mia ton sabbaton' (one of [the] sabbaths) where 'mia' as 'one' is generally applied as a cardinal number in the Greek feminine gender. There the feminine 'one of sabbaths' is expressed uniformly as a common phrase through out all of the N.T. resurrection passages and describes a solemn day of soulful matrimony in reflection to the 'queen of sabbaths'.

These same sabbaths are stated in Leviticus 23:15 of the KJV where it says to count seven (week of) sabbaths between Passover and Pentecost. There the Greek word επτα as 'seven' is cardinal in meaning as well. Furthermore, the original Greek in Acts 20:7 with the breaking of bread is described as occurring 'on one of the sabbaths' after the days of unleavened bread in Acts 20:6 leading up to Pentecost in Acts 20:16. Similarly, our resurrected Lord reappeared before His disciples on different intervals of the weekly Sabbath within the same group of sabbaths i.e. 'μια σαββατων' of St. John 20:19.

 Thus too, the author for Mark 16:9 may have been describing the resurrection day occurring on the chief sabbath 'πρώτη σάββατου' (as being primary and pre-eminent in nature for the seventh day cycle of weekly rest) after the Sheaf Offering Day passed on Nisan 16th.

* The phrase on 'one of the sabbaths' = 'μιαν σαββατων' (partitive genitive) in the intermediate segment of Matthew 28:1 and all other resurrection verses generally refers to any one of the (seven weekly) sabbaths between Passover & Pentecost (i.e. Lev 23:15). There the resurrection day was presented on Saturday Nisan 23rd being the first weekly sabbath following the 2 high Sabbaths (Friday Nisan 15th & Thursday Nisan 21) of the Passover period. The same reasoning follows likewise to all the other Gospel's resurrection verses stated elsewhere in the New Testament. As for the actual times stated within the resurrection day itself, it is possible that Mary may have loitered lengthy around the tomb for a while.

In Matthew 28:1 the Greek word 'επιφωσκουση' is likely a reference of time late in the day before the evening light. Compare also to Luke 23:54 where 'επεφωσκεν' transliterated as 'epiphoska' describes the time of day just before the (high) sabbath was about to begin. The word there in the 'Latin Vulgate Text' is described explicitly as 'illucescebat'. Compare also to Psalms 148:3 "Praise ye him, sun and moon: praise him, all ye stars of light".

At; http://www.peshitta.org/ you may see the Aramaic equivalent as 'twilight' for Matthew 28:1.

Many commentators believe that the next new day in Jewish early reckoning was determined when 3 stars became visible in the night sky.

The Revised version 1881 states in Mark 16:2 that the 2 Marys came to the sepulcher 'when the sun was (already) risen' which could refer to a time late within the day before the sun was over the horizon. It may merely be a situation of interpreting the 'pluperfect verb' in the proper past tense with an accurate preconceived notion. This moment in time likely happening within the 11th hour (e.g. 4:00-5:00 p.m.) of the day.

Luke 24:1 makes reference to 'deep dawn' (TKI) possibly being the eve in the 12 hour (e.g. 5:00-6:00 p.m.) right before the next calendar day which began after sunset when 3 stars became visible in the nightly sky.

John 20:1 makes reference to Mary coming 'early (in anticipation) with darkness (next day) yet (to) being' (TKI). Thus being another instance of interpreting in the proper tense which redefines the moment as being an evening time late in the resurrection day.

People were allowed to travel on the Sabbath up to a .75 mile limit (i.e. Josh 3:3,4). Thus the Ladies would have rested for the most part (according to the commandment) on the Sabbath day then traveled to the tomb later in the day likely anticipating a burial anointment by candlelight after the Sabbath had passed. It is also possible that the ladies were aware of Joseph's visit to the tomb on the previous day of Friday.

Matthew 12:39.40 compares Yehoshua's body (physically) in the tomb as equivalent to the same duration of time for Jonah being (physically) in the belly of the whale.

Yehoshua's body was placed in the tomb in the evening on Wednesday Nisan 20th and resurrected (72 hrs.) later in the evening on Saturday Nisan 23rd.

Luke 24:13-34

"And, behold, two of them went (were going) that same day to a village called Emmaus, which was from Jerusalem about threescore furlongs...And it came to pass, that, while they communed together and reasoned, Jesus (Yehoshua) himself drew near, and went with them....And their eyes were opened, and they knew him; and he vanished out of their sight.... And they rose up the same hour, and returned to Jerusalem, and found the eleven gathered together, and them that were with them....Saying, The Lord is risen indeed, and hath appeared to Simon."

* Note the pluperfect tense indicates the sojourners returned within an hour's time of distance as permitted by restriction of a Sabbath day's journey.

Furthermore, The Gospel of Peter, The Gospel of Nicodemus, The Apostolic Constitutions, and the Didascalia Apostolorum all contain Passion narratives that can be resolved and accounted for with a common parity in Jewish chronology of a post Passover (feast) resurrection experience.

Where Passover Nisan 14th (full moon) fell on a Thursday, the integral group or week of weekly Saturday sabbaths leading up to a Pentecost (Saturday Sivan 6th) for the year AD 34 should have been; Nisan 23, Nisan 30, Iyyar 7, Iyyar 14, Iyyar 21, Iyyar 28, and Sivan 6th. There Yehoshua resurrected on a weekly sabbath (Nisan 23rd) after the Passover feast within a group of 7 integral Sabbaths (i.e. Lev 23:15).

* Note that these calculations are based similarly to the 'model' established by Hillel II (AD 367) where Nisan (Abib) has 30 days, Iyyar has 29 days, and Sivan has 30 days.

Thus the resurrection of our Lord Saviour likely occurred on Saturday May 1st, and the day of Pentecost arrived 43 days later on Saturday June 12th. The resurrection day on Saturday May 1st would have been the second Sabbath from the second full moon after the Vernal Equinox in AD 34 being the Hebrew 3794 year since recorded creation. Thus, the resurrection followed the crucifixion on Wednesday April 28 after the Passover day being on Thursday April 22nd in AD 34. These were real dates in the Julian calendar and are astronomically ascertained. Please see;

http://www.timeanddate.com/calendar/?year=34&country=34

Subsequently, the Church authorities at the Council of Nicaea AD 325 deemed to fix the date of the Lord's day in close proximity after the

Vernal Equinox (March 22nd – Julian Calendar) ruling Sunday as the day of adherence in an annual and weekly observation being the regulatory mainstream traditional practice ever since.

* However, such time has passed and many Christians believe that the reconstruction of the Holy temple is an essential undertaking before the second coming of our Messiah. What if the temple of mention is one in reference to a Spiritual movement of Christian believers who uphold the Sabbath day as the true Holy day? To those whom acknowledge the bodily temple of Yehoshua (Rev 21:22) being raised in a full glory to the fulfillment of terms as prescribed by the 'Sign of Jonah'. To those who recognize the true resurrection day occurring on a weekly Sabbath as the original Koine Greek shows.

However, what if we continue to worship and interpret the bible under the veil of sub-standard post Nicene traditionalism? Is it non-consequential? Does it not make any difference? Will we be sealed overall as a true congregation fit for the day, when our Blessed Messiah returns for His beloved bride?

"But pray that your flight be not in the winter, neither on the sabbath day." St. Matthew 24:20

That time may be very close indeed. May we all be alert. May we all be already.

Robert Young shows 'sabbaths' (σαββατων) as plural in 'Young's Literal Translation' and in his 'Analytical Concordance to the Holy Bible' for the resurrection verses where he believed and explains 2 sabbaths (Annual Nisan 15th & the weekly Saturday sabbath) coinciding simultaneously on the very same day between the crucifixion and resurrection of our Lord.

He believed in a Friday Nisan 14th crucifixion and a Sunday Nisan 16th (first fruits / Lev 23:11) resurrection.

His understanding of theology underlies him to say 'First' rationalizing Sunday as the next day after the 'sabbaths' (2 sabbaths that coincided together). The sense of understanding here is that the 'First Day' (Sunday) was ablative from the sabbaths. This seems to be the common thread between the traditional Biblical interpreters of the Greek references. They believe that 'the first of sabbaths'and Sunday are the same identical day. Also the phrase from Lev 23:15 has a sense in the word 'sabbaths' (heptad = a period of 7) x 7 as being interpreted to mean 'a week of weeks' (heptad x hepdomad) as understood in relation to Pentecost Sunday occurring annually year after year in the Civil calendar.

This is the typical reason why Robert Young and mainstream theologians justify in their logic that the 'first of sabbaths' must refer in meaning to 'the first day of the week'. This too may have been the reasoning justifiable to theologians during the times at the Council of Nicaea (AD~325) carried over to the Edict of Laodicea (AD~367) where the instilled Canon law # 29 says that Christians 'must work on the Sabbath'. The induction of fourth century replacement theology founded by 'Constantine the Great' was tolerated by the masses of Christians with unification to the Pagans (Sol Invictus & Mithraism) being in unison on the same weekly ground of 'Sun Day' worship.

Constantine took advantage of an opportunity to solidify a solution (Son day = Sun Day) for tolerance and harmony between the general masses of diverse religions within his empire.

Mainstream Christian theologians alike to Robert Young may have found difficulties in justifying logic behind scriptures pertaining to the 'Sign of Jonah' (Mth 12:39, 40 = 3 days & 3 nights) or the phrase 'after three days' (i.e. Mth 27:63 & Mrk 8:31) in order to fit a chronological gap between the crucifixion and resurrection time frame.

In their theological understanding, the 'Sign of Jonah' may have been considered merely as a metaphorical expression for the idiomatic phrase of '3 days and 3 nights'.It may only be to some late day interpreters of theology where the words of Yehoshua as "no sign given but the sign of Jonah" holds any deep merit to investigate literally in full analytical detail with profound implications there of. We can see that such a process runs deep through the souls of those who are convicted to lay it all out on the line. To those who firmly believe reprehensibly in 'the sign of Jonah' as also stated directly by Yehoshua himself (Mth 16:4; Luk 11:29, 30) and also mentioned in The Didascalia Apostolorum and The Apostolic Constitutions of the Holy Fathers.

Sec. 19 The Coverdale Bible 1535

Coverdale shows either 'one' or 'first' with 'Sabbath' or 'Sabbathes' in the resurrection verses from the Latin and German sources he used. This may suggest some form of indecisiveness or compromise on

Coverdale's part to oddly translate with ambiguity, however, the original Koine Greek sources show 'μια των σαββατων' which is transliterated as 'mia(n) ton sabbaton' as one consistent way only.

* All quotes are in the original English. (Quotes Begin)

"The Bible / that is, the Holy Scripture of the Olde and New Testament, faithfully and truly translated out of Douche and Latyn into Englishe. MDXXXV"

Matthew 28:1

"Upon the euenynge of the Sabbath holy daye, which dawneth ye morow of the first daye of ye Sabbathes, came Mary Magdalene and ye other Mary, to se ye sepulcre."

Mark 16:2

"And they came to the sepulcre vpo a daye of ye Sabbathes very early, wha ye Sonne arose."

Mark 16:9

"But Jesus (Yehoshua), whan he was rysen vp early vpo the first daye of the Sabbathes, he appeared first vnto Mary Magdalene, out of whom he cast out seun deuels."

Luke 18:12

"I fast twyse in the weke, I geue the tithes of all that I haue."

Luke 24:1

"Bvt vpon one of the Sabbathes very early in the mornynge, they came vnto the Sepulcre, and brought ye spyces which they had prepared, and certayne wemen with them."

John 20:1

"Vpon one daye of the Sabbath, came Mary Magdalene early (whe it was darke) vnto the sepulcre, sawe that the stone was take from the sepulcre."

John 20:19

"The same Sabbath at eue wha ye disciples were gathered together, and the doors were shut for feare of ye Jewes, came Jesus (Yehoshua), and stode I ye myddes, sayde vnto the: Peace be wit you."

Acts 20:7

"Vpon one of the Sabbathes , whan the disciples came together to breake bred, Paul preached vnto them, wyllinge to departe on the morow, and contynued the preachinge vnto mydnight."

1 Corinthians 16:2

"Vpon some Sabbath daye let euery one of you put aside by him selfe, and laye vp what so euer he thinketh mete, that the collection be not to gather whan I come."

Colossians 2:16

"Let no man therefore trouble youre consciences aboute meate or drynke, or for a pece of an holy daye, as the holy daye of ye new mone, or of the Sabbath dayes."

(Quotes End)

The Bible / that is, the Holy Scripture of the Olde and New Testament, faithfully and truly translated out of Douche and Latyn into Englishe. MDXXXV, Published by; A Ministry of The Bible Reader's Museum

Sec. 20 Parting the Ways

A close examination of Matthew, Mark, and Luke does reveal that Yehoshua (Jesus) with His disciples fulfilled the Passover Seder ceremony on Nisan 15 being the 'πρωτη ημερα των αζυμων' = 'first day of unleavened (bread)' as described from Matthew 26:17,20,21 ; Mark 14:12,17,18 ; Luke 22:7,14 giving reference to the night of the nation's preservation which commemorated the Israelite's former departure to freedom from slavery in Egypt.

Furthermore, St Paul's wonderful statement; "Purge out therefore the old leaven, that ye may be a new lump, as ye are unleavened. For Christ are Passover is sacrificed for us: Therefore let us keep the feast, not with old leaven (Nisan 14), neither with the leaven of malice and wickedness; but with the unleavened bread (Nisan 15-21) of sincerity and truth."

1 Corinthians 5:7,8

After carefully reviewing the Old Testament scriptures you will see that the Passover lamb was slaughtered on Passover Nisan 14 in the late afternoon when the sun was setting down. The Passover lamb was to be consecrated with unleavened bread on the nightly beginning of Nisan 15. Any remains were to be sacrificed to God Almighty (i.e. Ex 12:10) and to be consumed by fire before morning.

Colossians 2:16 "Let no man therefore judge you in meat, or in drink, or in respect of an holy day, or of the new moon, or of the sabbath (σαββατων) days: Colossians 2:17 Which are a shadow of things to come; but the body is of Christ."

Paul's statement is a defense of the Apostles' non-continuance of clinging to the former regulatory ordinances behind their strict adherence to the Passover Seder with the observation of unleavened bread taking on a new meaning with the sanctity of Yehoshua's shed blood and body.

Paul then refers to the body of Christian believers through Yehoshua's achievement who are given their direct guidance through the Holy Spirit's discernment regarding such matters. Thus, the former law under hand written ordinances had been replaced wholly by the gift of the Holy Spirit's presence in governing all believer's discretion at will.

The key point being that the atonement behind our Lord's sacrifice was paid and fulfilled completely. Our salvation was obtainable, and the Holy Spirit would now come as a comforter to preserve and guide all Christian believers in every way regarding all matters of truth.

However remitted and longstanding, Jews through history have continued to look backwards by commemorating their Passover lamb on the nightly beginning of Nisan 15. There the symbolized elements of the

Seder are ingested in a ritual type cleansing of purification for God's preservation.

Jews continuing in the ways of these ordinances through the old covenant practices have not yet acknowledged the atonement for sin paid through Yehoshua's redemption.

** Transparently the Church transcended through the murky ages of the first three centuries while Christians endured a test of cruelty beyond any comparison. Christians were spurned, ridiculed, and tortured to barbaric deaths for not confessing allegiance to the Imperial throne. There large gatherings in public arenas were held on a Sunday mass scale exhibiting the spilled blood of Christians with animals alike. There the new forming Church was transcending on the blood of Christian Martyrs.

The Eastern Church up until the mid-second century commemorated the death and resurrection of Yehoshua along with the annual Jewish Passover festival as taught by the late Apostle John and claimed by his loyal observing followers. This position as observed by the Church of the East created a conflict with the Church of the West around AD ~155 which became known as the Quartodeciman Controversy. After much debate, Bishop Victor of the West by a consensus of presupposition would over rule to dismiss the traditional observation of Passover by the Church of the East as represented by Bishop Polycarp from Ephesus.

Please see; http://en.wikipedia.org/wiki/Quartodecimanism

The Christian Church by the fourth century would claim 'by God's authority' to defect from Sabbath observation by congregating on

Sunday as a way of avoiding any further religious contentions with the Jews.

Thus a legal recognition for Christians would patronize the specified reforms stipulated under 'Constantine the Great' where Christians were allotted the 'first day of the week' for Sunday worship in lieu of the Lord's Day no longer recognized on the Jewish weekly Sabbath.

* Note - Constantine decreed on March 7, 321 'dies Solis' as the day of the sun, being Sunday, the Roman day of rest: (Quotes Begin)

"On the venerable day of the Sun let the magistrates and people residing in cities rest, and let all workshops be closed. In the country however persons engaged in agriculture may freely and lawfully continue their pursuits because it often happens that another day is not suitable for grain-sowing or vine planting; lest by neglecting the proper moment for such operations the bounty of heaven should be lost." (Quotes End)

Codex Justinianus, lib. 3, tit. 12, 2; Philip Schaff, History of the Christian Church, Vol. 3 / 5th ed. New York: Scribner, 1902 pg 380, note 1

See; http://en.wikipedia.org/wiki/Sol_Invictus See also; http://en.wikipedia.org/wiki/Helios

Later at the Council of Nicaea (AD 325) the attending Bishops unanimously solidified that Easter would be annually commemorated on the first Sunday from the first full moon after the Vernal Equinox (March 22nd), and the majority of books in the Old and New Testament would begin to come together for the Canonization of the Holy Bible as we know it today. It was then that Church authorities considered to which books were kept and of which books were not.

However, the Bible became complete when Athanasius the Bishop of Alexandria made a more concrete decision on the matter with 65 books for the Old & New Testament at the council of Laodicea AD 364. Furthermore, it wasn't until AD 419 that the final decision was reached at the fourth Council of Carthage to allow the book of Revelation to be added into the Bible works after some prolonged debates. However, many uncanonized books like The Apocryphal Gospel of St. Peter (fragments), 'The Gospel of Nicodemus', 'The Constitutions of the Holy Fathers' or 'The Didascalia (Syriac) Apostolorum', all with a Passion testimony are absent from the bible works because they were not classified as first handed testimonies from eye witness accounts of the Gospel events.

Unfortunately, the 'continuity' and pertinent details between these outside books compared along with the Gospel books of the bible has been commonly overlooked by a majority of theological scholars.

* Furthermore, the establishment of Church Canon laws at the Edict of Laodicaea (AD~363) made it clear that Christians were to segregate specifically away from Jewish practices having no collaboration as such in anyway whatsoever.

Canon law 29 says that Christians 'must work on the Sabbath'.

See:http://www.ccel.org/ccel/schaff/npnf214.viii.vii.iii.xxxiv.html

Canon law 37 says that it is 'unlawful to share festal provisions' from Jews.

See;

http://www.ccel.org/ccel/schaff/npnf214.viii.vii.iii.xlii.html

Canon law 38 says that is 'unlawful for Christians to receive unleavened bread' from the Jewish Passover.

See; http://www.ccel.org/ccel/schaff/npnf214.viii.vii.iii.xliii.html

* Some rights were unattainable to common peoples but were a privilege to church leaders as seen in Canon law 16 where 'the Gospels and Bible books were read on the Sabbath'. See; http://www.ccel.org/ccel/schaff/npnf214.viii.vii.iii.xvii.html

The vast majorities of peoples were uneducated and illiterate through the 'Dark Ages' and were unauthorized to possess a bible in any way. Bibles were not published for common peoples until the much later times of the sixteenth century. Christian practices established from those Canon laws became a traditional setting with a trend for more Church laws to follow. Reformation brought indifference but a tolerance between various doctrines survived in the long run.

Our Lord's resurrection day may be determined by the timing of His last Passover in the events as portrayed in the Bible along with certain Passion books that were not included. As time surpasses, more comparable information becomes obtainable, and modern communication spreads yesteryears' reality more rapidly.

Is it too late for a formal re-evaluation of the Passion events? Has our interpretation of biblical history from the past served us well? Do we possess the academical, spiritual, and moral obligation to be sure of this? Like one Song Artist has sung;

"The answer my friend is blowin' in the wind, the answer is blowin' in the wind". (Song lyric Quote of B. Dylan 1962)

Sec. 21 Constantine's Mandatory Christian Compliance to Sunday Worship

 * The institution of Sunday Church worship was likely conceived through the influenced regime of Constantine the Great (Pontifex Maximus) whose historical imprint from the Sunday decree in AD 321 to the Council of Nicaea in AD 325 remains strong binding to worldwide Christian denominations of this present modern day. Subsequently, an ill transformation of the scriptural resurrection passages took on a whole new changed meaning in conforming to the degrees made authoritative by the 4th century state Church. Though Yehoshua claimed to be 'the Lord of the Sabbath' the entangled Church became forcibly intertwined with the Empire's mandatory shift in adopting the Sunday policy as the select day of religious worship.

These historical changes occurred primarily due to the Gentile's anti-semitic views holding the succession of Jewish populace as being responsible for the death of the Savior Yehoshua. Thus it seemed fittingly for Gentile Church leaders to segregate Christian believing people away from any association with Jewish religious practices, and to establish a newly formed separate Christian identity integrated on side with Sunday pagan worship. Sun-day as the venerable day hallowed to the Sol Invictus cult being highly honored by Gaius Flavius Valerius Constantinus as the key perpetrator in the initial birth of Sunday Christian fellowship.

Eusebius of Caesarea being a counterpart to Constantine's regime with a reputation as the Church librarian would re-work the Gospels where the phrase 'the first (prima) of the sabbaths' would appear later in Latin. Some centuries later William Tyndale would shift 'mia ton sabbaton' of the original Greek text in Acts 20:7 to read as;

(Quotes Begin) "on the morowe after the saboth" ,and in 1 Corinthians 16:2 to follow as "Vpon some sondaye" (Quotes End), in his 1534 English (second) edition. (ibid see section 32)

Subsequently, many other translations of the bible would follow where the original intended meaning behind the 'resurrection passages' would become eradicated. Thus, Christianity adapted 'the first day of the week' policy where the Nicene premise enveloped slowly into scripture. Thus likely, a deliberate tactic of 'eiosogesis' had ensued wrongly replacing the original hidden segments of the Holy Word for a lack of truth with a false representation of disinformation in the mistranslated Gospel resurrection passages.

The Koine (common) Greek phrase 'μια των σαββατων' in all the N.T. scriptural resurrection passages is trans-literated as 'mia ton sabbaton' and is literally translated as 'one of the sabbaths' but would be grammatically changed, and repeatedly misinterpreted to read as 'the first day of the week'. Only a few late literal translations or exact word for word interlinear bibles might come close to showing 'one of the sabbaths' from 'μια των σαββατων' in the original Greek 'resurrection passages' due to the Translator's conscience of grammatical disciplinary principles.

However, these truths were not totally concealed, nor reserved to the confines of privacy for those sworn into quiet agency regarding such knowledge as a highly kept secret.

Aside to the subversive old guard fraternities held in high self-esteem, the time has now come collectivey to spare this resourceful information to the common knowledge of all peoples, and to reclaim the Passion narrative of Yehoshua as regarded through the original Greek written Jewish testimonies of the initial founding Church Forefathers.

The 'Sabbath' practice for Christians was formally (not officially) changed to the 'first day of the week' by a clandestine controlling authority for a new rising Church. This was accomplished by the Roman Emperor 'Constantine the Great' (AD 321 – 325) and not from an earlier conception as Dr. Richard Challoner (1691-1781) or St. John Chrysostom (AD 347–407) may have believed. See clearly Challoner's footnote comments regarding Acts 20:7 'the first day of the week' for the breaking of bread in the Doway Reims N.T. Bible.

(Quote Begins)

"this change was undoubtedly made by the authority of the Church." (Quote Ends) (see web link) >

http://www.archive.org/stream/holybibletransla00chalrich#page/121/mode/1up

Sec. 22 A Lesson In Hermeneutics

* The interpretation behind the resurrection verses must take into account many factors in determining the proper meaning as intended by

the various authors all reporting the same event. Here are comments regarding such a process;

A GRAMMAR OF THE NEW TESTAMENT GREEK BY ALEXANDER BUTTMANN Andober : WARREN F. DRAPER, PUBLISHER. MAIN STREET 1880

TRANSLATOR'S PREFACE (Quotes Begin Pg.v)

"The day has gone by, indeed, when the extravagant maxim could find acceptance, "The better grammarian, the worse logician and theologian ;" but the somewhat indinscriminate depreciation of the study of the dead languages at the present day is not without injurious influence upon those who are preparing themselves to be expounders of the Divine Word. Even in that land which is reputed to be the home of philological studies, the prince of New Testament expositors has recently said : "We theologians are still far too deficient in a comprehensive and positive knowledge of Greek Grammar." (Meyer's Commentary / Pref. p. vii note)

"The sense of such a deficiency which the general progress of linguistic science must sooner or later awaken, and especially the recognition (which the growing tendency to break away from traditional opinions will force upon theologians) of the need of taking a new inventory of the biblical data, as preliminary to a revision of the scientific statements of the Christian faith, will eventually secure a welcome....."

J.H. Thayer- English Translator / Editor. (Quotes of original Author continues ... Pg. xiii , xiv)

" Nowhere, however, do the opinions of interpretors diverge more widely then where a knowledge of grammatical principles was wanting, and consequently the caprice of the private understanding had free course, so the often N.T. Grammar was made responsible for the strangest hypothesis and chimeras. Although the knowledge of grammar is not the only, still it is the primary and the main, foundation of interpretation ; at any rate, it is a check to subjective caprice and inordinate excesses. Without the foundation there can be no talk about certainty in explaining the Scriptures ; for we possess no inspired interpretation."

"Linguistic products, even the most sacred, are like all others, subject to the restraint of linguistic laws, which, be they ever so special, are nevertheless Laws, which every author spontaneously and unconsciously obeys. To establish such definite laws, together with the just as definitely – limited exceptions (so far forth as the latter either rest upon analogies in ordinary usage, or at least group themselves together under a distinctly traceable special analogy) and to combine all these phenomena into one systematic whole, is the business of a special grammar.in"

" Many passages of scripture , however, are of such a kind that, owing to the limited extant of the several books, they are destitute of any other analogy. These, to be sure, must then be explained from themselves, from the context and the tenor of Scripture or by the aid of ancient tradition (which must have for us the greater authority the nearer it stands to to the time of composition of the Scriptures), in a word, historically rather than grammatically."

"Such cases must be left principally to Exegesis. If Grammar notices them, it does so rather incidentally, and for the sake of completeness ; their value to Grammar can only be determined by their relation to analogies already established. For she can adopt, and work up solid portions of the system she would found, only those results of Hermeneutics which rest upon analogies, if she will not run the risk of being compelled to pull to pieces tomorrow what she today perhaps has laboriously built up, and to cast away as useless material what she has over-hastily made the corner pillar of her structure."

"On the other hand, it would be just as erroneous, if she in haughty self sufficiency should wish utterly to seclude herself from the results of Hermeneutics. Both sciences must continually go hand in hand. As Hermeneutics has in Grammar her constant monitor and the touchstone of her results, so Grammar receives from the discreet critical- historical inquiry of Exegesis perpetually new enrichment. It is an unscientific, irrational demand, – and one which misjudges man's powers, – that one science should not begin to act till after the other has finished its work ; since, on the contrary, they are both at the same time called and commissioned for the understanding of the Scriptures. By progressive discernment, with the help of Grammar and under the guidance of critico-historical research, continually to diminish the number of passages which refuse to submit to any linguistic analogy (and consequently as to whose meaning commentators generally diverge in all directions) is one of the leading and abiding aims of Hermeneutics." (All Quotes End)

AXEXANDER BUTTMANN (Author) POTSDAM, Nov. 1858

A GRAMMAR OF THE NEW TESTAMENT GREEK

See Online at;

http://www.archive.org/stream/cu31924021607159#page/n7/mode/2up

Furthermore...(Quote Begins)

"There can be no biblical theology unless it is based on sound biblical exegesis, and there can be no sound biblical exegesis unless a firm textual and grammatical foundation has been laid for it."

(Quote Ends) F.F. Bruce, Head of the Department of Biblical History of Literature in the University of Sheffield

September 1952 Pg. x in the fore text of 'W.E. Vine's Expository of New Testament Words'

Thomas Nelson Publishers, New York, 1985

* It is evident that much critical debate is necessary to partake of the screening process in resolving that of which seems to be the most difficult unintelligible passages.

Sec. 23 The Sabbath Precedence

Hebrews Chapter 4 -KJV (Quotes Begin)

1."Let us therefore, fear lest, a promise being left us of entering into His rest, any of you should seem to come short of it."

2. "For unto us was the gospel preached, as well as unto them: but the word preached did not profit them, not being mixed with faith in them that heard it."

3. "For we which have believed do enter into rest, as He said, As I have sworn in My wrath, if they shall enter into my rest, although the works were finished from the foundation of the world."

4. "For He spake in a certain place of the seventh day on this wise, And God did rest the seventh day from all his works."

5. "And in this place again, If they shall enter into My rest."

6. "Seeing therefore it remaineth that some must enter therein, and they to whom it was first preached entered not in because of unbelief:"

7. "Again, he limiteth a certain day, saying in David, To day, after so long a time; as it is said, To day if ye will hear His voice, harden not your hearts."

8. "For if Joshua had given them rest, then would he not afterward have spoken of another day."

9. "There remaineth, therefore a rest to the people of God."

10. "For he that is entered into His rest, he also hath ceased from his own works, as God did from his."

11. "Let us labor therefore to enter into that rest, lest any man fall after the same example of unbelief."

12. "For the word of God is quick, and powerful, and sharper than any two- edged sword, piercing even to the dividing asunder of soul and spirit,

and of the joints and marrow, and is a discerner of the thoughts and intents of the heart."

13. "Neither is there any creature that is not manifest in his sight: but all things are naked and opened unto the eyes of him with whom we have to do."

14. "Seeing, then, that we have a great high priest, that is passed into the heavens, Jesus (Yehoshua) the Son of God, let us hold fast our profession."

15. "For we have not an high priest which cannot be touched with the feeling of our infirmities; but was in all points tempted like as we are, yet without sin."

16. "Let us therefore come boldly unto the throne of grace, that we may obtain mercy, and find grace to help in time of need." (Quotes End)

Sec. 24 The Passion Month and Year

Many online Luni-Solar Metonic 19 year cycle calendars are based on Hillel II's (AD~367) intercalary regulated principles for the sake of diaspora. Therefore showing earlier calendar years reformed to the later methods based on Hillel's trajectories calculated in reverse order.

The Sacred calendar in temple days was governed and controlled by the Sanhedrin council whose duty was to observe the lunar cycles in the night skies. The calendar records from those years were probably lost in the fall of Jerusalem (AD~69). I have also examined possible dates and years through modern astronomical programs that mathematically calculate time in reverse precession for moon cycles after the Vernal Equinox (March 22nd – Julian Calendar) in search of an applicable Passion year.

 The subject for following lunar cycles in search of a probable crucifixion year is also discussed at pertaining lengths in the;

'Handbook of Biblical Chronology' by Jack Finegan (Revised Edition C. 1998 Hendrickson Publishers, Inc. ISBN 1-56563-143-9)

 See Pg. 363 Table 179 (Quotes Begin)

"As calculated by Fotheringham; (The year) AD 34 Nisan 14 fell on Mar 24 Wed and Nisan 15 fell on Mar 25 Thu." "Or, supposing the intercalation of a month in the preceding year, as shown by Parker and Dubberstein, so that Nisan came one month late, then Nisan 14 fell on April 22 Thu and Nisan 15 fell on Apr 23 Fri." (Quotes End)

 * Here below understand accordingly to the astronomical authorities of Parker and Dubberstein in their book 'Babylonian Chronology: 626 BC – AD 75' (Wipf & Stock Publishers May 2007

 ISBN- 9781556354533 – formerly published by the Brown University Press 1956 Pg. 1)

 (Quotes Begin)

"The calendar year was composed of lunar months, which began when the thin crescent of the new moon was first visible in the sky at sunset. Since the lunar year was about eleven days shorter than the solar year, it was necessary at intervals to intercalculate a thirteenth month...astronomers began to recognize, as the result of centuries of observations of the heavens, that 235 lunar months have almost exactly the same number of days as nineteen solar years. This meant that seven lunar months must be intercalated over each nineteen-year period."

(Quotes End)

* Thus with the intercalation of an added month of Adar II along with the previous month of Adar I we have the most likely occurrence of Nisan 15th falling on a Friday April 23rd, AD 34 (Julian) in the 3794 year with a 'Passion' narrative to follow.

In a Passover (Nisan 14) of Thursday April 22nd AD 34 the crucifixion likely followed on Wednesday April 28th (Nisan 20), a resurrection on Saturday May 1st (Nisan 23), the day of ascension on Wednesday June 9th (Sivan 3), and the day of Pentecost on Saturday June 12th (Sivan 6). These dates are shown in Hebrew and Julian calendar times.

See the 2 modern online calendar sites below that mathematically calculate astronomical time in reverse precession for moon cycles after the Vernal Equinox;

http://www.timeanddate.com/calendar/moonphases.html?year=34&n=110

http://www.timeanddate.com/calendar/?year=34&country=34

There in the year AD 34 the calendar authorities 'Parker and Dubberstein' in 'Babylonian Chronology' (Pg. 46) determine Nisan 1 landing on a Friday April 9th.

Subsequently, Nisan 15th would land on Friday April 23rd with a formative 'Passion' narrative to follow.

* Note – The actual cycle for moon appearances is days where there is 354 days in 12 months. The lunar calendar comes up 11.25 days shorter then the solar calendar at 365.25 days. The need for Luni-Solar calendar regulation was established by Hillel II to make up later where the Sanhedrin Council was non-existent.

The accuracy of pin-pointing dates of major events around Yehoshua's time is most difficult. Thus being, that all public records were lost, or covered up, and the Sanhedrin's former practices in hind-sight of routine calendar intercalation are relatively speculative.

In actual reality, the accuracy of placing a Passion event into a specific calendar year by Lunar observation may be possibly out by a month depending on the intercalary methods practiced by the Sanhedrin Council at that time.

The Sanhedrin Council observed the ripeness and readiness of the barley crop to determine the availability of produce for the first fruits sheaf offering dedication day. If the crop was not ripe enough the chances for an intercalary (leap) month would be instituted.

Astronomers determine accurately by reverse precession that full moons occurred after the Vernal Equinox (March 22) where Passover Nisan 14th may have occurred on Friday April 7th AD 30, Tuesday March 27th AD 31, Wednesday April 25th AD 31 (after an intercalary month), Monday April 14 AD 32, Friday April 3rd AD 33, Wednesday March 24th AD 34, Thursday April 22nd AD 34 (after an intercalary month), Monday April 11th AD 35, or Saturday March 31st AD 36. With all being said, modern methods of calculation are based accurately on reconfigured astronomy, however, the Passion event was likely fulfilled after an intercalary (leap) month of Adar II being added on to the preceding Adar I calendar month. The likeliness of the Passion event following an intercalary month will be discussed later in the next chapter.

Some scriptural passages suggest the crucifixion day occurred during a total eclipse of the sun (i.e. Luk 23:45) but reverse calculated astronomical statistics show that those findings were relatively inconsistent on a full moon near after the Vernal Equinox between the years of interest from AD 30 to AD 36. The likeliness then was probably a condition of high winds (e.g. ripping the temple curtain) stirring up the desert sands creating a distorted image of the sun visually comparable to a solar eclipse.

For online solar eclipses in years surrounding Jesus (Yehoshua's) passion event see; Maps-05-pdf, Plate 243; http://eclipse.gsfc.nasa.gov/SEpubs/5MCSE.html

Partial lunar eclipses on years surrounding Yehoshua's passion occurred on full moons of Wednesday April 25th 31 CE at 11:02 p.m. (probably on Nisan after an intercalary month of Adar II), and also on Friday April 3rd 33 CE at 5:38 p.m. that was only visible from Indonesia. A penumbral lunar eclipse occurred on Wednesday March 23rd 34 CE at 6:03 p.m.. Theologians have suggested the crucifixion event occurring on any one of those dates showing such a celestial phenomenon, however, a blood red appearance of the moon in a clear sky is only visible during a total eclipse.

For an online description of visual appearances with various lunar eclipses surrounding Yehoshua's Passion year, you may visit;

http://eclipse.gsfc.nasa.gov/LEcat5/LE0001-0100.html

* Note the various details and times when such occurrences happened.

For possible dates surrounding Yehoshua Passion, you may navigate around the various years by visiting;

http://www.timeanddate.com/calendar/?year=0031&country=34

* Note on site the bottom legend for moon phases.

Consider also at the beginning of Yehoshua's ministry where St. Luke 3:1 reads, "Now in the fifteenth year of the reign of Tiberius Caesar..." (Luk 3:21) has been attributed to a time in the summer of AD 29 from Tiberius' independent succession on August 19th AD 14. The likelihood of Yehoshua's resurrection occurring on the Passover of AD 30 would account for about a 1 year ministry and about a 2 year ministry in AD 31, so on and so forth. However, the Gospels make reasonable references to 5 consecutive Passovers (e.g.) as follows; (1) St. John 2:13, explicitly in AD 30. (2) St. Luke 6:1, connected inadvertently in AD 31. (3) St. John 5:1, implicitly in AD 32. (4) St. John 6:4, explicitly in AD 33. (5) St. John 12:1, explicitly in AD 34. A 4 years plus duration for Yehoshua's ministry is conceivably tangible where all four Gospel's periphery details must be in agreement when taken into account.

Therefore, Yehoshua would have been almost thirtyfive years of age at the time of the crucifixion in AD 34 from a likely beginning of His ministry in the early summer of AD 29 where Luke 3:23 reads;

"And Jesus (Yehoshua) himself began to be about thirty years of age..."

Thus an approximate age from a time supposing He was born in the 2 BCE year. Yehoshua was born in the summer when Shepherds were grazing their sheep (i.e Luk 2:8). The wise men followed the star of Bethlehem (i.e. Mth 2:2, 7, 9). A visual phenomena compounded by the orbital conjunction of Venus and Jupiter's binary paths in a visual alignment appearing as an emanating bright light through the night earthly skies of June 17th, 2 BC.

Please see the online article below for a detailed celestial evaluation of the Nativity event;

http://www.suite101.com/content/the-science-of-thechristmas-star-a9687

Thus Yehoshua was less than 1 year in age before King Herod's death in 1 BC where Josephus indicates in 'The Antiquities Of The Jews' XVII,vi,4, that Herod the Great died near after a (total) eclipse of the moon (Jan 10th) and before a Passover Nisan 14th full moon occurring on April 8th of the 1 BC year.

To view lunar eclipses for the astronomical 0000 year (equivalent to 1 BC) in table 04821 at bottom of score, visit;

http://eclipse.gsfc.nasa.gov/LEcat5/LE-0099-0000.html

It was then that all children under 2 years of age living in Bethlehem were exterminated by King Herod's insane attempt to remain in control as stated by Matthew 2:16.

Please Note – Technically, it is difficult to find any celestial phenomenon between the years of 7 BC to 1 BC to support a nativity event occurring around Bethlehem on December 25th. (See NASA)

In the traditional belief, scholars are divided between a Passover Nisan 14 crucifixion occurring on a Friday April 7 after the full moon technically occurring on April 6 at 7:34 p.m. on AD 30 or some believe in a crucifixion moment occurring with a Friday full moon technically appearing at 2:34 p.m. on April 3 of AD 33. Some believe as well in a crucifixion occurring on a Wednesday afternoon before the Passover full moon appeared technically at 10:02 p.m. after sunset (6 pm.) on April 25th AD 31 but really as the next day in Jewish reckoning. Some believe in a crucifixion moment occurring on a Wednesday March 24 AD 34 slightly following a full moon appearing on Tuesday of March 23rd technically at 5:28 p.m. in AD 34.

In Matthew 21:18 and Mark 11:13 we read about a hungry Yehoshua condemning a tree being non-existent in figs at a fruit bearing time when it was expected to be.

In Matthew 24:32, Mark 13:28 and Luke 21:30 we read about the observation of fig shoots resembling a time closely near summer. All of these biblical accounts were in a time leading up to Yehoshua's last Passover.

Were these the indications of a late Passover cycle likely due to the embolism of an intercalary month of Adar II being added on to the month of Adar I preceding the Passover month of Nisan (Abib)?

On the contrary, did Yehoshua condemn a fig tree too early when the natural growing cycle to bear fruit had not been acquired?

The likeliness of a preceding intercalary month of about 30 days would necessitate some further growing time as an essential maturation for the ripening of the 'breba crop' (spring bearing fruit ripening later after dormancy thru winter from the previous year's growth) in these scriptural passages.

Therefore an intercalary month as Adar II would have likely been added by the Sanhedrin Council to prolong the growing season where Nisan 14 (full moon) would have been deferred further along in the AD 34 year onto Thursday April 22nd with a full moon technically occurring at 9:43 a.m..

* Note – Sir Isaac Newton (1642-1727) may have reasoned (allegedly) to a Passion event with a late Passover Nisan 14 occurring on a Thursday April 22nd in AD 34 after identifying the set scriptural passages regarding the recorded scenes of nature in all of the Gospels. Thus an evaluation determined by him, yet possibly overlooked through the eyes of many bible scholars.

See an online calendar;

http://www.timeanddate.com/calendar/?year=34&country=34

Note bottom legend for moon phases.

http://www.timeanddate.com/calendar/moonphases.html?year=34&n=110

* Note precise times of full moon appearances. You may navigate to surrounding years of interest.

If the preceding Passover cursing of the fig tree event occurred on the day of the lamb procurement (Nisan 10th) thus might have been either; Monday April 3rd AD 30, Saturday April 21st AD 31, Thursday April 10 AD 32, Monday March 30th AD 33, Saturday March 20th AD 34, or tangibly later (after an intercalary month) on Sunday April 18th in AD 34.

Likewise, another scriptural account in Luke 6:1 shows a resonable time within Yehoshua's ministry after the second Passover (AD 31) where the heads of grain were ripe enough to eat when the growing season was deferred and matured.

* Note – the KJV authors interpret the produce there as corn in meaning, however, in actuality as kernels of grain and not maize that came by Columbus from the Americas at a much later time. However, an intercalary month would have pushed Passover Nisan 14th (full moon) on to a Wednesday April 25th AD 31 when the growing season matured long enough to yield a new fresh crop harvest. If that moment happened on the 'first weekly sabbath after the second day being Thursday Nisan 16th the date for wheat availability may have been on Nisan 17th as Saturday April 28th in AD31. To see the wheat harvest in Israel visit;

http://www.zimbio.com/pictures/ht0wjSaeeub/Wheat+Harvest+Begins+In+Israel

However, If the author (Luk 6:1) had intended to describe 'the second sabbath after the first sabbath being Saturday Nisan 17th, the date for Yehoshua to pick the grain may have been on Nisan 24 as Saturday May 5th in AD 31. (Julian Time).

The Koine Greek words ' ενσαββατω δευτεροπρωτω' in reference to the Sabbath at Luke 6:1 is shown as the 'second chief ' (1207) in the Interlinear Bible (Sovereign Grace Publishers) in conjunction with the Strong's (numbered) Greek Concordance. Miles Coverdale translated his 1535 Bible from Latin and German (Martin Luther) sources where he shows the English phrase as the 'second principal Sabbath'.

At a much later time we see the Apostles (Acts 20:7) breaking bread on 'μια των σαββατων = one of the sabbaths' (CLT). This occasion occurring on a sabbath 'after' the days of unleavened bread (Acts 20:6), and 'before' Pentecost (Acts 20:16). Thus being on 'one sabath of a week = seven integral weekly sabbaths' (e.g. Lev 23:15) between Passover and Pentecost.

Sec. 26 Fulfilment of Bible Prophecy

With the potential fulfilment of Bible prophecy we will account for all the years between 445 BC (reconstruction of the holy temple) to AD 2022 (completion of Daniel's 70th week).

Daniel Chapter 9 vs.23-26 (Quotes Begin-KJV)

23. "At the beginning of thy supplications the commandment came forth, and I am come to shew thee; for thou art greatly beloved: therefore understand the matter, and consider the vision."

24. "Seventy weeks are determined upon thy people and upon thy holy city, to finish the transgression, and to make an end of sins, and to make reconciliation for iniquity, and to bring in everlasting righteousness, and to seal up the vision and prophecy, and to anoint the most Holy."

25. "Know therefore and understand, that from the going forth of the commandment to restore and to build Jerusalem unto the Messiah the Prince shall be seven weeks, and threescore and two weeks: the street shall be built again, and the wall, even in troublous times."

26. "And after threescore and two weeks shall the Messiah be cut off, but not for himself: and the people of the prince that shall come shall destroy the city and the sanctuary; and the end thereof shall be with a flood, and unto the end of the war desolations are determined."

(Quotes End)

Daniel's vision has been interpreted under various methods of calculation from the time beginning with the rebuilding of the second temple by Nehemiah in 445 BC to a later tangible crucifixion year in the 'cutting off ' of the Messiah. Hence, an interpretation by inclusive reckoning counts 7+60+2 = 69 individual Sabbatical release year periods (Shemitah) every 7 years as shown by using 'Benedict Zuckermann's' charts (pgs. 60 & 61) as a compilation from recorded historical references where 135 BC, 37 BC, AD 69, and AD 1175 were ascertained as known Sabbatical years.

'A Treatise on the Sabbatical Cycle and the Jubilee': A Contribution to the Archaeology and Chronology of the Time Anterior and Subsequent to the Captivity by Benedict Zuckermann (trans. A. Lowy; London: Chronological Institute, 1866; repr. New York: Sepher Hermon Press, 1974 ISBN O-87203-044-X

445 B.C. (Temple Rebuilding Instruction)

444/443 B.C. 1st Sabbatical Year* (Neh 10:31)

437/436 B.C. 2nd Sabbatical Year

430/429 B.C. 3rd Sabbatical Year

423/422 B.C. 4th Sabbatical Year

416/415 B.C. 5th Sabbatical Year

409/408 B.C. 6th Sabbatical Year

402/401 B.C. 7th Sabbatical Year

395/394 B.C. 8th Sabbatical Year

388/387 B.C. 9th Sabbatical Year

381/380 BC 10th Sabbatical Year

374/373 BC 11th Sabbatical Year

367/366 BC 12th Sabbatical Year

360/359 BC 13th Sabbatical Year

353/352 BC 14th Sabbatical Year

346/345 BC 15th Sabbatical Year

339/338 BC 16th Sabbatical Year

332/331 BC 17th Sabbatical Year

325/324 BC 18th Sabbatical Year

318/317 BC 19th Sabbatical Year

311/310 BC 20th Sabbatical Year

304/303 BC 21st Sabbatical Year

297/296 BC 22nd Sabbatical Year

290/289 BC 23rd Sabbatical Year

283/282 BC 24th Sabbatical Year

276/275 BC 25th Sabbatical Year

269/268 BC 26th Sabbatical Year

262/261 BC 27th Sabbatical Year

255/254 BC 28th Sabbatical Year

248/247 BC 29th Sabbatical Year

241/240 BC 30th Sabbatical Year

234/233 BC 31st Sabbatical Year

227/226 BC 32nd Sabbatical Year

220/219 BC 33rd Sabbatical Year

213/212 BC 34th Sabbatical Year

206/205 BC 35th Sabbatical Year

199/198 BC 36th Sabbatical Year

192/191 BC 37th Sabbatical Year

185/184 BC 38th Sabbatical Year

178/177 BC 39th Sabbatical Year

171/170 BC 40th Sabbatical Year

164/163 BC 41st Sabbatical Year

157/156 BC 42nd Sabbatical Year

150/149 BC 43rd Sabbatical Year

143/142 BC 44th Sabbatical Year

136/135 BC 45th Sabbatical Year* (Josehus Antq.of Jews)

129/128 BC 46th Sabbatical Year

122/121 BC 47th Sabbatical Year

115/114 BC 48th Sabbatical Year

108/107 BC 49th Sabbatical Year

101/100 BC 50th Sabbatical Year

94/93 BC. 51st Sabbatical Year

87/86 BC. 52nd Sabbatical Year

80/79 BC. 53rd Sabbatical Year

73/72 BC. 54th Sabbatical Year

66/65 BC. 55th Sabbatical Year

59/58 BC. 56th Sabbatical Year

52/51 BC. 57th Sabbatical Year

45/44 BC. 58th Sabbatical Year

38/37 BC. 59th Sabbatical Year *(Herod's siege of Jerusalem)

31/30 BC. 60th Sabbatical Year

24/23 BC. 61st Sabbatical Year

17/16 BC. 62nd Sabbatical Year

10/9 B.C.. 63rd Sabbatical Year

3/2 B.C... 64th Sabbatical Year (Messiah's celestial birth)

+ 5/6 A.D....65th Sabbatical Year

+ 12/13 AD. 66th Sabbatical Year

+ 19/20 AD. 67th Sabbatical Year

+ 26/27 AD. 68th Sabbatical Year

+ 33/34 AD. 69th Sabbatical Year (Messiah cut off in AD 34)

+ 68/69 AD.* (Known Sabbatical Years all shown * with asterisks)

* Note 1 BC goes directly into AD 1 without a 0 calendar year.

7) BC 3/2 Sabbath Year

1) BC 2/1
2) BC 1/1 AD
3)   1/2 AD
4)   2/3 AD
5)   3/4 AD
6)   4/5 AD
7)   5/6 AD Sabbath Year

* Sabbatical (Shemitah) years (i.e. Lev 25:4-7; Deut 15:1,9,12; Neh 10:31; Jer 34:14) were referred to as release periods (every seventh year) where debts were forgiven, sacrifices happened, and the fields lay fallow to replenish the earth. Here within the cycle span of combined agricultural years they are measured from autumn Fall / Tishri to Tishri / autumn Fall season overlapping the adjoining Civil calendar (Jan 1 - Dec 31) years. Thus, the Passion event of the Messiah Yehoshua occurred on the 69th Sabbatical year of AD 34 'after' the edict order was granted by Persian King Artaxerxes 1 Longimanus to Nehemiah in returning to Jerusalem for the actual rebuilding of the second temple on the month of Nisan in 445 BC.

For further applicable resources refer to; SABBATICAL

YEARS, JUBILEES, AND PRIESTLY COURSES (Sec.

224) in the 'Handbook of Biblical Chronology' by Jack Finegan Revised Edition C. 1998 Hendrickson Publishers, Inc. ISBN 1-56563-143-9

http://books.google.ca/books?ei=8ZUFTbaoEoujnweA7LnlDQ&ct=result &id=bHYUAQAAIAAJ&dq=Handbook+of+Biblical+Chronology&q=release

Secondly, another less common interpretation of Daniel's 69 weeks for the 'cutting off of the Messiah' requires mathematical calculations to consider AD 31 as a possible year for Yehoshua's crucifixion. Here we have 69 (7+60+2) x7 (week) = 483 years x 360 (days allegedly in a prophetic year) = 173,880 days / 365.25 (days in a solar year) = 476 (solar years) – 445 BC (Nehemiah's rebuilding of second temple) = AD 31.

There the full moon after the Vernal Equinox (March 22nd) occurred on Tuesday March 27th at 12:58 p.m. AD 31 or on a Wednesday April 25th (after an intercalary month) at 10:02 p.m. AD 31 in Jerusalem time. See AD 31 moon chart;

http://www.timeanddate.com/calendar/moonphases.html?year=31&n=110

* Thirdly, another uncommon interpretation of Daniel's 69 weeks for the 'cutting off of the Messiah' requires mathematical calculations to consider AD 30 as a possible year for Yehoshua's crucifixion. Here we have 69 (7+60+2) x7 (week) = 483 years x 354 (days in a lunar year) = 170,982 days / 360 (days allegedly in a prophetic year) = 475 (alleged solar years) – 445 BC (Nehemiah's rebuilding of second temple) = AD 30.

The Passover full moon after the Vernal Equinox (March 22nd) occurred on Thursday April 6th at 9:15 p.m. AD 30. The Passover lamb could have been sacrificed the next afternoon on Friday April 7th AD 30.

See AD 30 moon chart;

http://www.timeanddate.com/calendar/moonphases.html?year=30&n=0

Fourthly, in another interpretation some theologians claim the Lord was 'cut off ' in AD 31 from the start of His ministry supposing it began in AD 27 'after' 483 (7+60+2×7) solar years from an edict announcement to Ezra by Persian King Artaxerxes 1 Longimanus in 457 BC granting permission to Jews that lived formerly under Babylonian exile to return freely on to Jerusalem. However, after a delayed start, many Historians agree that the actual temple rebuilding followed later on Nisan of 445 BC when Nehemiah returned to Jerusalem.

Thus, an overall broad examination to Yehoshua being crucified and raised on any of the years from AD 30, AD 31, AD 32, AD 33, to an early Passover of AD 34 (without an intercalary month) has limited proportionate details.

Daniel 9:25

"Know therefore and understand, that from the going forth of the commandment to restore and to build Jerusalem unto the Messiah the Prince shall be seven weeks, and threescore and two weeks: the street shall be built again, and the wall, even in troublous times."

*Note here that "even in troublous times" may be a standard length of time measured as 'seven weeks and threescore and two weeks' being interpreted as equal to a total of 69 x 7 (sabbatical years) = 483 years.

Daniel 7:25

"And he (Constantine the Great) shall speak great words against the most High, and shall wear out the saints of the most High, and think to change times (the actual Lord's day) and laws (the Sabbath

Commandment): and they (the Church) shall be given into his hand (authority) until a time and times and the dividing of time."

*Note here that "time and times and the dividing of time" may be referring to 1+2+.5 = 3.5 x 69 x 7 (Sabbatical years) = 1690.5 years from AD 325 (being Constantine's desecration of our Lord's Sabbath changed to the weekly pattern of following Easter Sunday) bringing us out to the 2015.5 year.

* Note that; 2 BC (our Lord's birth), AD 34 (our Lord's crucifixion), AD 321 (Constantine's Sunday Decree), AD 328... 2001 (the 9/11 event), and 2008 (the USA financial collapse), occurred all coincidentally on Sabbatical years.

Daniel 9:27

"And he (Constantine the Great) shall confirm the covenant with many for one week (i.e. a week of years; AD 322, AD 323, AD 324, AD 325, AD 326, AD 327 AD 328 etc): and in the midst of the week (AD 325) he shall cause the sacrifice (our Lord's Day) and the oblation (the Sabbath rest) to cease, and for the overspreading of abominations he shall make it desolate, even until the consummation, and that determined shall be poured upon the desolate

* May it be considered that the unsealed vision of Daniel 9:24 is referring to the eschatological 'seventieth week' (as a 7 year period) coming near fulfilment after Elul 29 = Sunday September 13 of the 2014/2015 Sabbatical Year beginning on Tishri 1 of the 2015/2016 year of Jubilee and ending on Elul 29 of the 2021/2022 Sabbatical Year?

* Consider also statements from the Book of Revelation with an added chronological interpretation in relation to Daniel;

Revelation 11:2

"But the court (Church) which is without the (bodily) temple (of Yehoshua) leave out (in the AD 34 Sabbatical year), and measure it not; for it is given unto the Gentiles: and the holy city (the fall of Jerusalem in the AD 69 Sabbatical Year) shall they tread under foot (until the) forty and two months (42nd Sabbatical release year period = AD 321)."

* Hence there were exactly 42 Sabbatical release year periods starting with our Lord's crucifixion in AD 34 as part of the first Sabbatical Year and ending in AD 321 as the closing part marking the forty second Sabbatical Year when the Edict of Constantine the Great began his official change to the emphasis of pagan Sun-day observation.

AD. 33/34 1st Sabbatical Year *(Messiah's bodily temple was cut off)

AD. 40/41 2nd Sabbatical Year

AD. 47/48 3rd Sabbatical Year

AD. 54/55 4th Sabbatical Year

AD. 61/62 5th Sabbatical Year

AD. 68/69 6th Sabbatical Year *(Temple Destruction at Jerusalem)

AD. 75/76 7th Sabbatical Year

AD. 82/83 8th Sabbatical Year

AD. 89/90 9th Sabbatical Year

AD. 96/97 10th Sabbatical Year

AD. 103/104 11th Sabbatical Year

AD. 110/111 12th Sabbatical Year

AD. 117/118 13th Sabbatical Year

AD. 124/125 14th Sabbatical Year

AD. 131/132 15th Sabbatical Year

AD. 138/139 16th Sabbatical Year

AD. 145/146 17th Sabbatical Year

AD. 152/153 18th Sabbatical Year

AD. 159/160 19th Sabbatical Year

AD. 166/167 20th Sabbatical Year

AD. 173/174 21st Sabbatical Year

AD. 180/181 22nd Sabbatical Year

AD. 187/188 23rd Sabbatical Year

AD. 194/195 24th Sabbatical Year

AD. 201/202 25th Sabbatical Year

AD. 208/209 26th Sabbatical Year

AD. 215/216 27th Sabbatical Year

AD. 222/223 28th Sabbatical Year

AD. 229/230 29th Sabbatical Year

AD. 236/237 30th Sabbatical Year

AD. 243/244 31st Sabbatical Year

AD. 250/251 32nd Sabbatical Year

AD. 257/258 33rd Sabbatical Year

AD. 264/265 34th Sabbatical Year

AD. 271/272 35th Sabbatical Year

AD. 278/279 36th Sabbatical Year

AD. 285/286 37th Sabbatical Year

AD. 292/293 38th Sabbatical Year

AD. 299/300 39th Sabbatical Year

AD. 306/307 40th Sabbatical Year

AD. 313/314 41st Sabbatical Year

AD. 320/321 42nd Sabbatical Year *(Constantine's Sunday Decree)

Revelation 13:5

"And there was given unto him (Constantine the Great) a mouth speaking great things and blasphemies; and power was given unto him to continue (through) forty and two months (from Sabbatical release AD 321 year period to present)."

* God's prophetic timetable is measured here exclusively in individual Sabbatical release year cycle periods only.

Sec. 27 The Sheaf Offering – Calculation to Pentecost

My comments I would like to make here is about the 'sabbath' mentioned in Leviticus 23:11, 15. It is from this Sabbath that determines the correct day that the wave offering (Sephira Omer) and the day of Pentecost (Shabuoth/Shavuoth) would fall on for each particular year.

There has always been much debate amongst theologians about which Sabbath ?? is being referred to in the passage of Leviticus 23:11, 15.

Leviticus 23:11 reads;

"And he shall wave the sheaf before the Lord, to be accepted for you: on the next day after the sabbath (??) the priest shall wave it."

Leviticus 23:15 reads;

"And ye shall count unto you from the morrow after the sabbath (??) from the day that ye brought the sheaf of the wave offering; seven sabbaths shall be complete:"

One interpretation is that the Sabbath as stated pertains to the Saturday (seventh day) weekly sabbath with in the Passover period. There the Omer count would commence the next day on Sunday and Pentecost would always arrive 50 days later on a Sunday year after year regardless to whatever calendar # date it landed on. This practice was started by the Sadducees who happened to be the majority of temple priests in Yehoshua's time.

Another common interpretation was that the 'sabbath' in Leviticus 23:11, 15 is the Nisan 15th high Sabbath in the Passover period which could land on a different week day year after year. There the Omer count would begin the next day on Nisan 16th (wave offering) where the 50 day count could arrive on the third consecutive month of Sivan 6th on a different weekday year after year. There they number the omer from the time the sickle hits the barley (Deut 16:9), and not consistently from where Sunday lies in the Passover period. Whatever day of the week that Nisan (Abib) 16th landed on they would put the sickle to the barley when it was ripe, and the counting of 50 days would begin immediately.

This was the known practice of the Pharisees who handed it down through the oral law in generation after generation where the majority of common people practiced this observation which is commemorated by the Jews through all times to our present modern day.

The 70 LXX authors (Pharisees) of the Septuagint Greek Old Testament (~250 BC) wanted to clarify matters so they took liberty by taking out the word 'sabbath' in Leviticus 23:11 and replacing it with the phrase; 'the morrow after the first day' but they left the word 'sabbath' in Leviticus 23:15. This was done to assimilate the 'sabbath' in verse 15 as the 'first day' mentioned in verse 11. The words 'first day' in verse 11 signifying the 'first day' of the Passover feast which was always identified and recognized as Nisan 15th being a 'high sabbath' observed on 'the first day of unleavened bread'.

Let me add that Nisan 14th was regarded as Passover 'eve' and never regarded as the 'first day' of the Passover feast. Thus being a vast misinterpretation by those who commonly reference the beginning of Nisan 14th as a feast day.

However, the name 'Passover' was loosely and commonly regarded as an 8 day celebrated observation beginning on Nisan 14th the eve to the 15th inclusive to the end of Nisan the 21st as mentioned by Josephus the Jewish historian (AD~70)(i.e. Antiq., Bk 2, Ch 15, L 315-7)

Another point is that Paul identifies himself in Acts 23:6, 26:5 as a Pharisee who had a major influence in association with the Apostles indicates that they likely recognized the 'sabbath' of Leviticus 23:11 as the high day sabbath of Nisan 15th. This practice was observed as well by the disciples and our Lord who was often at wits end towards the Sadducee sect. (i.e. Mrk 12:24)

 * Some people believe in a Wednesday Nisan 14th crucifixion of Yehoshua with a Saturday Sabbath resurrection on Nisan 17th which they believe to be the first sabbath of a series of 7 (i.e. Lev 23:15) sabbaths leading up to Pentecost.

From a resurrection standpoint occurring on a Saturday Nisan 17th to another time of 40 days later we would arrive on the day of ascension. That day could have been a Wednesday the 26th on the second consecutive month of Iyyar where our resurrected Lord commissioned the Apostles as shown in Acts 1:5-8.

If you interpret here the 50 day counting of Pentecost commencing from the day 'after' Nisan 15th being the (High) Sabbath as the first day of unleavened bread (as interpreted from Leviticus 23:11, 15), Pentecost could arrive on a Friday 6th in the third consecutive month of Sivan. Pentecost here could arrive 9 days later after the day of ascension.

Other believers interpret the 'sabbath' of Leviticus 23:11, 15 as the weekly Saturday Sabbath on the Passover period in the same time frame as shown previously. There the counting commences on Sunday Nisan 18th where the 50 day count completes on a Sunday Sivan 8th which could have been 11 days later after the day of ascension being on a Wednesday Iyyar of the 26th.

From the Traditional resurrection standpoint occurring on a Sunday Nisan 16th to another time of 40 days later we could arrive on the day of ascension. That day could have been on Thursday the 25th in the second month of Iyyar. If you interpret here the 50 day counting of Pentecost commencing from the day 'after' Saturday Nisan 15th (Lev 23:11, 15), Pentecost could have arrived on a Sunday 6th in the third consecutive month of Sivan. Pentecost here could have arrived 10 days later after the day of ascension.

In a post Passover resurrection scenario Yehoshua is crucified on Wednesday Nisan 20th, and raised on the Saturday sabbath of Nisan 23rd, where the day of ascension occurs 40 days later on a Wednesday Sivan 3rd, and Pentecost arrived only 3 days later on the Saturday sabbath of Sivan 6th, from where the 50 day count commenced from the beginning of Saturday Nisan 16th, after the (High) sabbath on Friday Nisan 15th being the first day of unleavened bread.

** Yehoshua did say in Acts 1:5 to the disciples on the day of ascension that the promised gift of the Holy Spirit would follow in a short time later.

"... but ye shall be baptized with the Holy Ghost not many days hence." KJV

"... but in a few days you will be baptized with the Holy Spirit." NIV

* As you can see from each belief a different time frame becomes established after 40 days from the resurrection in the words of Yehoshua spoken on the day of ascension as 'not many' or 'a few' equating to a different number of days in waiting until the Holy Spirit made God's Spirit filled presence present on the day of Pentecost in Acts 2:1-5.

This is intriguing where the waiting period of either 9, 10, or 11 days from the day of ascension to the day of Pentecost would be amassed when Yehoshua said quite clearly to the number of days being 'not many' (KJV) or 'a few' (NIV) in Acts 1:5.

* Note that the calculations made above are based on the model established by Hillel II (AD 367) where the Hebrew months of Nisan similarly has 30 days, Iyyar has 29 days, and Sivan has 30 days. If the Sanhedrin Council in Yehoshua's time counted 30 days from the second consecutive month of Iyyar, it is possible that Pentecost landed on Sivan 5.

* Note – The probability of the 'Sheaf Offering Dedication' (Abib/Nisan 16th) occurring on a Sabbath day was very tangible as revealed from within the fourth century rabbinical writings such as the Tosefta/Menahot (tractrate 10:23) that was aimed to supplement the Mishnah. Please See;

http://books.google.com/books?id=HjosAAAAIAAJ&q=Menahot+10:23&dq=Menahot+10:23&ie=ISO-8859-1&output=html&cd=9

http://books.google.com/books?id=oOOJVr7Cu78C&pg=PA103&lpg=PA102&dq=Menahot+10:23&ie=ISO-8859-1&output=html

Leviticus 23:14 "And ye shall eat neither (the new grains) bread, nor parched corn (kernels), nor green ears, until the selfsame day that ye have brought an (first fruits) offering unto your God: it shall be a statute for ever throughout your generations in all your dwellings."

Deuteronomy 16:3 "Thou shalt eat no leavened bread with it; seven days (Nisan 15. 16, 17, 18, 19, 20, 21) shalt thou eat unleavened bread therewith…"

Deuteronomy 16:8 "Six days (Nisan16, 17, 18, 19, 20, 21) thou shalt eat (the new grain) unleavened bread…"

* On Nisan 15 Jews ate unleavened bread made from the 'old grain'. Jews ate unleavened bread (barley loaf) from the 'new grain' for six days beginning from Nisan 16 – Nisan 21. This way works consistently when the first fruits offering was presented at the beginning of Nisan 16th after the Nisan 15 'high Sabbath' regardless to whatever week day it fell upon for each particular year.

However, if the omer counting was intended after the 'weekly Sabbath' occurring on a Nisan 19, the First fruits offering might have begun on Sunday Nisan 20 in a peculiar way. Jews might have ate unleavened bread from the 'old grain' for five days on Nisan 15, 16, 17, 18, 19 and unleavened bread (barley loaf) from the 'new grain' for two days beginning on Nisan 20 and Nisan 21. The numbers of days for the eating of unleavened bread from the old produce or the new produce would vary accordingly to each different year if the first fruits offering were modeled after the 'weekly Sabbath' when ever it occurred in the Passover period.

Deuteronomy 16:3 says 'seven days' and 16:8 says 'six days' when unleavened bread was to be eaten. The only reconciliation here for each consecutive year was that new grain could NOT be eaten until the 'first fruits offering was presented on the beginning of Nisan 16 after the Sabbath (i.e. Lev 23:11) being the high day of Nisan 15 regardless of whatever week day it fell upon in each particular year. Thus unleavened bread was observed on the first day made from the old grain and on the following six days made from the new grain for a combined total duration of seven days.

See also; The Apostolic Constitutions of the Holy Fathers (A.D. 375) –
Book V Chapter XVIII. (Quote Begins)

"Do you therefore fast on the days of the Passover, beginning from the
second day (Nisan 16th) of the week (feast-period) until the preparation
(Nisan 20th), and the Sabbath (Nisan 21st) , six days (Nisan 16, 17, 18,
19, 20, 21) making use of only bread, and salt, and herbs, and water for
your drink." (Quote Ends)
Translated from 'Greek' by William Whiston and was revised and
reprinted by Irah Chase, D.D. D. Appleton & CO. New York 1840

Joshua 5:10 "And the children of Israel encamped in Gilgal, and kept the
passover on the fourteenth day of the (Abib / Nisan) month at even
(sunset) in the plains of Jericho."

Joshua 5:11 "And they did eat of the old corn (kernels) of the land on
the morrow (Nisan 15) after the passover, unleavened cakes, and
parched corn (kernels) in the selfsame day."

Joshua 5:12 "And the manna ceased on the morrow (Nisan 16) after
they had eaten (Nisan 15) of the old corn (kernels) of the land; neither
had the children of Israel manna any more; but they did eat of the (first)
fruit of the land of Canaan that year."

* Here the time scale is given in reference to the high Sabbath of Nisan
15th (Lev 23:11), and not the consistency of a weekly Sabbath on a civil
calendar 7 day week. Thus Joshua 5:12 is in line with the first fruits
being consistently offered annually on the 16th day of the Abib / Nisan
month regardless to whatever day of the week it could land upon for
each particular / individual solar lunar year. Consecutive years very,

when the full moons appear ever changing, on different week days year after year.

.

.

Sec. 28 A Summary of the Passion Chronology

* Note – All dates are in context of the Hebrew and Julian calendars.

* Note – Unmarked scriptural quotes are in the KJV.

– Yehoshua was born in the summer of the 2 BC Sabbatical (Shemitah) year when Shepherds were grazing their sheep (i.e. Luk 2:8). It was then that the supposed 3 wise men followed the bright burning star (i.e. Mth 2:2, 7, 9). That being a visual phenomena compounded together by an in depth conjunction of Venus and Jupiter's planetary paths in a binary alignment emanating a bright ray of light around the night earthly skies of June 17th, 2 BC (NASA).

- Yehoshua was less than 1 year in age before King Herod's death in 1 BC where Josephus indicates in 'The Antiquities Of The Jews' XVII,vi,4, that Herod the Great died near after a total eclipse of the moon (Jan 10th-NASA) and before a Passover Nisan 14th full moon occurring on April 8th of the 1 BC year.

– Yehoshua's ministry likely begins in the early summer of AD 29 where St. Luke 3:1 reads;

"Now in the fifteenth year of the reign of Tiberius Caesar..." has been attributed from Tiberius' independent succession beginning on August 19th, AD 14.

– The five consecutive Passovers (Pesach) in the New Testament Gospels portraying Yehoshua's 4 years plus ministry were;

St. John 2:13, 23 explicitly in AD 30.

St. Luke 6:1, inadvertently in AD 31.

St. John 5:1, implicitly in AD 32.

St. John 6:4, explicitly in AD 33.

St. John 12:1, explicitly in AD 34 being the Hebrew 3794 year.

– Yehoshua and the disciples arrive in Bethany (old location) on Friday Nisan 8th, April 16 AD 34 being 'six days before the Passover' (full moon) on Thursday Nisan 14th. (i.e. Jhn 12:1)

– Yehoshua makes a triumphant entry in to Jerusalem on a colt on the Saturday Sabbath of Nisan 9th, April 17th AD 34. (i.e. Jhn 12:13-15)

– The cursing of the fig tree occurred after an intercalary (added) month when the breba crop of figs were in maturity, and the upsetting of the money changers took place on the day of the lamb procurement being Sunday Nisan 10th, April 18th in AD 34.(i.e. Ex 12:3; Mrk 11:12-15)

– The Nisan Passover full moon followed the embolism of the Adar II (intercalary month) on Thursday of April 22nd being technically at 9:43 a.m. in AD 34. There Yehoshua and the disciples met for a casual anticipatory Passover gathering starting on Nisan 14th (i.e. John 13:1) in the late afternoon with a foot washing cleansing ritual 'before the feast' at sundown.

http://www.timeanddate.com/calendar/?year=34&country=34

* See bottom legend for moon phases.

– Yehoshua and the disciples partake of a genuine Passover Seder on the First day of unleavened bread as a high Sabbath (commemorating the Jewish forefather's former anticapatory departure from Egypt) on the nightly beginning of 'Good Friday' (Good Day =Yom Tov) Nisan 15th, April 23rd, AD 34.

(i.e. Mth 26:17- 21 Mrk 14:12-18, Luk 22:7-21)

– The temple priests present the first fruits barley offering (e.g. Tosefta/Menahot/tractrate 10:23) on the weekly sabbath of Saturday Nisan 16th, April 24th AD 34 (i.e. Lev 23:11). Here the 50 day omer count commences from this day forward.

– Yehoshua and His disciples meet for the last supper on the end (eve) of Sunday Nisan 17th as the third day in the Passover feast just prior to the nightly beginning of Monday Nisan 18th as the fourth night of unleavened bread in the 'Didascalia Apostolourum'.

– There He was incarcerated later to Annas, Caiaphas then examined by Herod of Antipas, Pilate the Governor, and was subjected to the Sanhedrin Judiciary Council for an apparent due legal process in customary accordance to Jewish law.

Matthew 27:15

"Now at that feast (Nisan 15-21) the governor was wont to release unto the people a prisoner, whom they would."

Mark 15:6

"Now at that feast (Nisan 15-21) he released unto them one prisoner, whomsoever they desired."

Luke 22:1

"Now the feast (Nisan 15-21) of unleavened bread drew nigh, which is called the Passover."

Luke 23:17

"For of necessity he must release one unto them at the feast (Nisan 15-21)."

– A realistic time lapse of about 60 hrs. incurred through 3 consecutive days of Jewish reckoning starting with a Nisan 18th night (second watch) arrest to a Nisan 20th afternoon (sixth hour) crucifixion allowing for the events of Yehoshua being before Annas, Caiaphas, Herod Antipas, Pilate on a few occasions, the Sanhedrin Council on a couple occasions, and the appeal before the vast throngs of crowds on a couple of separate occasions.

– Yehoshua may have stood trial in a non-publicized daytime hearing on Monday as the fourth day of the feast being Nisan 18th, and was convicted to death on the fifth day of the feast being Tuesday Nisan 19th, all occurring within the secularized days of the Passover feast. e.g. 'Tractrate Sanhedrin' (4:1 Danby) & 'The Didascalia Apostolorum'.

– Yehoshua was first seen by Pilate on a Tuesday morning (Jhn 18:28) with much disputing to follow. On Wednesday morning He was flogged in a mock-type crucifixion manner at 9 am. in the 3rd hour (Mrk 15:25). He was then seen lastly by Pilate and expelled by the the Sanhedrin Council to be literally crucified in the 6th hour (Jhn 19:14) at 12pm.

"Because thereon they crucified Me, in the midst of their festival of unleavened bread, as it is said of old in David: In the midst of their festivals they set their signs, and they knew not [Ps 74.4 (73.4 LXX)]."

(Quotes End) 'The Didascalia Apostolorum' shown as [Ps 74.4 (73.4 LXX])

"Keep your nights of watching in the middle of the days of unleavened bread. And when the Jews are feasting, do you fast and wail over them, because on the day (Nisan 20) of their feast they crucified Christ; and while they are lamenting and eating unleavened bread in bitterness, do you feast."

(Quotes End) 'The Apostolic Constitution of the Holy Fathers Sec. III Book V Chap XVII

– The crucifixion occurred on the preparation (secular) day of Wednesday Nisan 20th, April 28, AD 34, that drew prior to the great (high) Passover Sabbath of Nisan 21st being the last day of the feast of unleavened bread. There, Yehoshua's body is covered over with a 1 piece purchased garment and placed in a tomb for a quick rash burial.

(i.e. Jhn 19:31, Mrk 14:51, Luk 23:53)

– Yehoshua would have been almost thirty five years of age at the time of the crucifixion in AD 34 from a likely beginning of His ministry in the early summer of AD 29 where Luke 3:23 reads;

"And Jesus (Yehoshua) himself began to be about thirty years of age..."

Thus an approximate age from a time supposing He was born around June 17 (celestial event) in the summer of the 2 BCE year. (Note the 1 BC year goes directly into AD 1 with no 0 calendar year.)

– The prophecy of Daniel was fulfilled when the Messiah was cut off on the crucifixion day in Nisan of the 69th (AD 34) Sabbatical release year 'after' an edict was granted with permission from the Persian King Artaxerxes 1 to Nehemiah for the actual restoration of the second temple at Jerusalem in 445 BC.

(i.e. Dan 9:25, 26, 27; Lev 25:4-7; Mth 27:50)

– The final Seventh day of unleavened bread was a high Sabbath (ending the feast commemorating the Israelite fore-father's deliverance in passing out of Egypt) on Thursday of Nisan 21st, April 29th, AD 34. (e.g. Mrk 16:1)

— Pilgrims return home on Friday of Nisan 22nd, April 30th, AD 34 after 'the last day of unleavened bread' while the disciples were distraught in bereavement.

(i.e. 'The Gospel of Peter' – Verse 12)

— The home preparations of ointments by the women occurred separately along with a meticulous customary burial of Yehoshua's body by Joseph (under guarded watch) being on the secular day of Friday Nisan 22nd, April 30th, AD 34 after the high sabbath (i.e. Mrk 16:1) and before the weekly sabbath (i.e. Luk 23:5) e.g. 'The Gospel of Nicodemus'). The strips of linen and headdress are rediscovered on the resurrection day by Peter in St. John 20:5.

— The resurrection of our Lord Savior occurred on 'one of sabbaths' from 'μίαν σαββάτων' transliterated as 'mian sabbaton' or 'μια των σαββάτων' transliterated as 'mia ton sabbaton' being on the weekly sabbath of Saturday Nisan 23rd, May 1st, AD 34. (i.e. Mth 28:1, Mrk 16:2, Luk 24:1, Jhn 20:1, in the Koine Greek Texts).

— 'The sign of Jonah' was fulfilled literally when the resurrection occurred '3 days & 3 nights' (3 x 24 hrs. = 72 hrs.) from the crucifixion day (i.e. Matthew 12:39/40, 'The Apostolorum Didascalia', 'The Apostolic Constitutions of the Holy Fathers', and "After three days I will rise again." Mth 27:63, Mrk 8:31)

— Thus an evening resurrection occurring on 'one of sabbaths' (a Greek partitive genitive case function) being Saturday Nisan 23rd (the first weekly sabbath after the 2 High Passover Sabbaths had completed) within a heptad group of 7 weekly sabbaths being; Saturday Nisan 23rd as May 1st in AD 34, Saturday Nisan 30th as May 8th in AD 34, Saturday

179

Iyyar 7th as May 15th in AD 34, Saturday Iyyar 14th as May 22nd in AD 34, Saturday Iyyar 21rst as May 29th in AD 34, Saturday Iyyar 28th as June 5th in AD 34, and Sivan 6th as June 12th in AD 34 after the Passover First Fruits (Saturday Nisan 16th) from the First day of unleavened bread (Friday Nisan 15th high sabbath).

(i.e. Lev 23:11,15, 16)

– The resurrection day on Saturday May 1st would have been the second Saturday from the second full moon after the Vernal Equinox (March 22nd) in AD 34 being the Hebrew 3794 year since creation.

– The resurrected Yehoshua reveals himself on 'one of sabbaths' to His disciples and eight days later (on one of the sabbaths) along with Thomas being on the Sabbath Saturday of Nisan 30th, May 8th, AD 34. (i.e. Jhn 20:19, 26)

– The day of ascension occurred on Wednesday of Sivan 3rd, June 9th AD 34 as 40 days from the resurrection day. (i.e. Acts 1:3-5)

– The day of Pentecost (Shabuoth – Shavuoth) being the infilling of the Holy Spirit arrived on the Saturday Sabbath of Sivan 6th, June 12th AD 34 being 50 days from the first fruits offering, 43 days from the crucifixion day, and only 3 days ("in a few days" NIV) after the day of ascension. (i.e. Acts 2:1; Lev 23:16, Deut 16:9, 10 ; 'The Gospel of Nicodemus')

– The Lord's day and the Holy Spirit's day of Pentecost occurred on the 3794 /AD 34 Sabbatical (Shemitah) year since recorded history in relevance of the hallowed 'Sabbath' of the sacred 7th cycle.

- A revolt led later by Emperor Hadrian against all Jews in the second century, along with the Gentile religious reforms of Emperor Constantine the Great in the fourth century, would succeed to change the main-stream Christian Church's 'Lord's Day' and fixed it unto the so-called 'first day of the week' policy which would further aid the Council of Laodicea 363 AD (Shemitah/Sabbatical Year) in abolishing any further recognition or credence to our Lord's emphasis on Sabbath observation as a Biblical non-priority.

– The Lord's day on the Sabbath along with the Holy Spirits' Baptism on the Sabbath Day of Pentecost was issued solely through GOD'S GRACE but became officially abrogated by Constantine the Great in the AD fourth century under his unified public agenda at the Council of Nicaea AD 325 in favor of civil calendar date fixing the Lord's day and the day of Pentecost events on to 'the first day of the week' as a tribute he inscribed of himself on a coin.

"To the unconquerable/invincible Sun."

Thus a complacency in Christianity was later stabillized further-more from Constantine's religious agenda through man's Canon laws established at the Council of Laodicea in AD 363 (Shemitah/Sabbatical Year).

-Transpiring   the Word of God by St. Jerome in AD 382 up to John Wyecliffe in AD 1380 for the resurrection verses gradually took on a whole new meaning in the the New Testament. There Yehoshua's (Jesus') resurrection on "one of the sabbaths" would be gradually twisted uneventfully to read as 'priman sabbati' (Latin as 'first sabbath') and later as 'the first day of the week'. Thus being the surviving status quo to universally fall in line with accommodating a mainstream focus on Constantine's monumental 'Sunday' vision to a Reformation floundering Church in general.

- Thus suppressing the original recognition of the hallowed weekly Sabbath for which both the Lord's Day and the Church's actual founding day of Pentecost had initially occurred. Thus unacknowledged as facts being compromised continously for nearly 1700 years in comparison to the applied commemoration of Sunday Church worship as affiliated with most wide stream denominations of Christianity today. Furthermore, the Jewish observation of Passover (Pascha) followed previously by Eastern Gentile Christians and Jewish Proselytes to Christianity was annulled by the early Western Church authorities being reduced to a hidden aid in gauging the true chronology behind the narrative event of Yehoshua's Passion.

- Subsequently many translations and versions of the Bible evolved over the past centuries and decades exhibiting 'the first day of the week' phrase throughout the resurrection verses contrary to the original intended Greek meaning.

- The changing of the Lord's Day from the Sabbath to Sunday came by a deliberate neo-Christianity fourth century order to segregate Christian religious ties away from Judaism as a political grab to gain a a stronger common widespread control over all of the multi-religious populace as a whole in general. As a result the official Lord's Day expression recognizd by main-stream Christianity became more dogmatic based, as an illusory belief, superficial in theory, other than from an authentic true historical account based soley on relevant factual information.

Sec. 29 Aftermath – a Timely Trip

It is well documented that Pilate served his 10 year term as the Roman Procurator of Judaea from AD 26 to AD 36. When the Yehoshua Passion story reached Rome it is rumored that Tiberius was very anxious for an official account of the event and immediately summoned Pilate to appear before him in Rome. However, Tiberius died before Pilate could reach Rome. It is well documented that Tiberius died on March 16th AD 37. It would also be reasonable to gage the traveling time by foot for a one way land trip of 2400 miles from Jerusalem to Rome or visa versa in the duration of 1 year or less. The first year was for the initial news of the Passion event to reach Rome safely. The second year was for Tiberius' summons to reach Pilate with a governor replacement in Jerusalem. The third year was for the escorted Pilate to reach Rome being a total of '3' years altogether.

Where a Passion event may have occurred in AD 30 there would have been a time lapse of about 7 years to Tiberius' death in AD 37. Thus Pilate's trip to Rome could have been delayed for about 4 years.

Where a Passion event may have occurred in AD 31 there would have been a time lapse of about 6 years to Tiberius' death in AD 37. Thus Pilate's trip to Rome could have been delayed for about 3 years.

Where a Passion event may have occurred in AD 32 there would have been a time lapse of about 5 years to Tiberius' death in AD 37. Thus Pilate's trip to Rome could have been delayed for about 2 years.

Where a Passion event may have occurred in AD 33 there would have been a time lapse of about 4 years to Tiberius' death in AD 37. Thus Pilate's trip to Rome could have been delayed for about 1 year.

Where a Passion event occurred in AD 34 there would have been a time lapse of about 3 years to Tiberius' death in AD 37. Thus Pilate's trip to Rome should NOT have been delayed in anyway whatsoever.

.

* Pegging the Passion event around that time can be determined by all of the periphery variables involved to sustain the proper year and month of the true Lord's Day.

Sec. 30 A Week of Sabbaths Observed

Here we have calculated the seven weekly Sabbaths of Lev 23:15 from 2 different source points as occurring between Passover to Pentecost with reference to the the Lord's Day on "mia ton sabbaton" literally stated as "one of the (seven) sabbaths (partitive genitive) in Mth 28:1, Mrk 16:2, Luk 24:1, & Jhn 20:1.

* The 7 weekly Sabbaths between Passover and Pentecost according to the Sadducees;

Leviticus 23:15

"And ye shall count unto you from the morrow after the (weekly) sabbath, from the (Sun) day that ye brought the sheaf of the wave offering; seven sabbaths shall be complete:"

Leviticus 23:16

"Even unto the morrow after the seventh sabbath shall ye number fifty days; and ye shall offer a new meat (Pentecost) offering unto the LORD."

Passover AD 31 Wed Nisan 14> Weekly Sabbath Nisan 17> Sunday Sheaf Offering Nisan 18> (1) Sat Nisan 24, (2) Sat Iyyar 1, (3) Sat Iyyar 8 (4) Sat Iyyar 15 (5) Sat Iyyar 22 (6) Sat Iyyar 29 (7) Sat Sivan 7 > Pentecost Sun Sivan 8.

Passover AD 34 Thur Nisan 14> Weekly Sabbath Nisan 16> Sunday Sheaf Offering Nisan 17> (1) Sat Nisan 23 (2) Sat Nisan 30 (3) Sat Iyyar 7 (4) Sat Iyyar 14 (5)Sat Iyyar 21 (6) Sat Iyyar 28 (7) Sat Sivan 6 > Pentecost Sun Sivan 7.

Passover AD 30 or AD 33 Fri Nisan 14> Weekly Sabbath Nisan 15> Sunday Sheaf Offering Nisan 16> (1) Sat Nisan 22 (2) Sat Nisan 29 (3) Sat Iyyar 6 (4) Sat Iyyar 13 (5) Sat Iyyar 20 (6) Sat Iyyar 27 (7) Sat Sivan 5 > Pentecost Sun Sivan 6.

The 7 weekly Sabbaths between Passover and Pentecost according to the Pharisees and the Apostle Paul;

Leviticus 23:15

"And ye shall count unto you from the morrow after the (high) sabbath (Nisan 15), from the day (Nisan 16) that ye brought the sheaf of the wave offering; seven sabbaths shall be complete:"

Leviticus 23:16

"Even unto the morrow after the seventh sabbath (or on) shall ye number fifty days; and ye shall offer a new meat (Pentecost) offering unto the LORD."

Passover AD 31 Wed Nisan 14> High Sabbath Thur Nisan 15> Fri Sheaf Offering Nisan 16> (1) Sat Nisan 17 (2) Sat Nisan 24 (3) Sat Iyyar 1 (4) Sat Iyyar 8 (5) Sat Iyyar 15 (6) Sat Iyyar 22 (7) Sat Iyyar 29 > Pentecost Fri Sivan 6.

☆ Passover AD 34 Thur Nisan 14> High Sabbath Fri Nisan 15> Sat Sheaf Offering Nisan 16 (1) Sat Nisan 23 (2) Sat Nisan 30 (3) Sat Iyyar 7 (4) Sat Iyyar 14 (5) Sat Iyyar 21 (6) Sat Iyyar 28 (7) Pentecost Sat Sivan 6.

Passover AD 30 or AD 33 Fri Nisan 14> High Sabbath Sat Nisan 15> Sun Sheaf Offering Nisan 16> (1) Sat Nisan 22 (2) Sat Nisan 29 (3) Sat Iyyar 6 (4) Sat Iyyar 13 (5) Sat Iyyar 20 (6) Sat Iyyar 27 (7) Sat Sivan 5 > Pentecost Sun Sivan 6.

These calculations are made where the Hebrew months of Nisan has 30 days, Iyyar 29 days, and Sivan 30 days.

The years AD 31 (D) and AD 34 (E) show Nisan after an intercalary month of Adar II in the appropriate season of years considering when Yehoshua picked kernels of wheat and later expected to find ripened fig fruit from the breba crop on the Sycamore tree during His last Passover visit to Jerusalem.

Note the admissions by the Apostle Paul and consider his mutual practices of sacred observation with the Apostles whom were formerly affiliated with Yehoshua;

Acts 23:6 "But when Paul perceived that the one part were Sadducees, and the other Pharisees, he cried out in the council, Men and brethren, I

(Paul) am a Pharisee, the son of a Pharisee: of the hope and resurrection of the dead I am called in question."

Acts 26:5 "Which knew me from the beginning, if they would testify, that after the most straitest sect of our religion I (Paul) lived a Pharisee."

See; Year 34 Calendar – Jerusalem
http://www.timeanddate.com/calendar/?year=0031&country=34

* Note the various appearances of moon phases. You may navigate to surrounding years of interest. (i.e. Nisan 14 AD 31 = Wed. April 25 or Nisan 14 AD 34 = Thurs. April 22).

* Note that many scholars presume the book of Acts was written by the same author as Luke, and Corinthians was written by Paul. There has been much debate amongst theologians regarding the authors of the Gospels whether the names of them correspond with the actual authors. For the most part it is agreed that the gospels were not written until the latter times of the first century.

Sec. 31 Epilogue

"But he answered and said unto them, An evil and adulterous generation seeketh after a sign; and there shall no sign be given to it, but the sign of the prophet Jonah:

For as Jonah was three days and three nights in the whale's belly; so shall the Son of man be three days and three nights in the heart of the earth." See St. Matthew 12:39,40.

Scripture is the divine Word of God and is able to be self-interpreted from within itself. All details must be accounted for where the pieces of tho Passion puzzlo must fit togothor fully. Man is not justifiod by omitting, obscuring, or adding to the Word as a means of redirecting believers away from God's plan. The Passion scriptures must be preserved in meaning as the Greek written Jewish authors had intended initially.

The hierarchy systems and evangelists of Christianity in this world today need to regain an insight on how they have swayed from the past. They need to come to terms, they need introspection, and they need to turn the page.

Why do you ask? To preserve the truth of the Gospels, and to give back a recognition in understanding to the identity of Christianity which has long since been compromised. To worship God commemorating the Passion event as it was presented in the beginning with a true meaning of divine integrity. Yehoshua rose on the Sabbath, plain and simple. The original Koine Greek scriptures tells us that. On His chosen SABBATH DAY, the power of God by Grace alone unleashed a wonderful preserving miracle of everlasting eternal life. Thus we are freely given a choice to embrace with our Heavenly Mentor in Spiritual unity with His perfect plan of Divine purpose and will. On that Sabbath Yehoshua entered His eternal rest. We too are given that option. See Hebrews 4: 9, 10, 11.

Sec. 32 Quotes and Further Things to Ponder

* Note all unmarked scriptural quotes are taken from the 1611 King James Version/KJV.

* * * Consider where William Tyndale's N.T. 'first' edition (1526) shows the Apostle's breaking of bread in Acts 20:7; (Quote Begins)

"On a saboth day the disciples came to gether for to break bread, and Paul preached unto them (ready to depart on the morrow) and continued the preaching unto midnight." (Quote Ends)

See online at; http://faithofgod.net/WTNT/acts_20.html

Consider also William Tyndale's N.T. "first' edition (1526) where the monies were already prepared for collection in 1 Corinthians 16:2; (Quote Begins)

"In some saboth day let every one of you put aside at home, and lay up whatsoever he thinketh meet, that there be no gatherings when I come." (Quote Ends)

See online at; http://faithofgod.net/WTNT/1_corinthians_16.html

THE NEW TESTAMENT – 1526 EDITION – TRANSLATED BY WILLIAM TYNDALE The British

Library 2000 (Hardbound) or Hendrickson 2009 (All Quotes End)

* The passages given here below regarding the Apostle Paul are stated directly from the MYLES COVERDALE BIBLE of 1535; (Quotes Begin)

Acts 20:7

"Vpon one of the Sabbathes , whan the disciples came together to breake bred, Paul preached vnto them, wyllinge to departe on the morow, and contynued the preachinge vnto mydnight."

1 Corinthians 16:2

"Vpon some Sabbath daye let euery one of you put aside by him selfe, and laye vp what so euer he thinketh mete, that the collection be not to gather whan I come." (Quotes End)

* * *

* Consider as well Thomas Cranmer's Great Bible of 1539 for THE ACTS OF THE APOSTLES' 20:7 which reads; (Quote Begins)

"And vpon one of the Saboth dayes, whan the disciples came together for to breake bread Paul preached vnto them (ready to departe on the morow) and continued the preachynge vnto mydnyght." (Quote Ends)

Pg. 793 The English Hexapla, London: Samuel Bagster & Sons 1861

***

Here we have statements from JEAN CALVIN'S Commentary on Matthew, Mark, Luke – Volume 3 (Quotes Begin).

Matthew 28:1

"Now in the evening of the Sabbaths, which began to dawn towards the first of the Sabbaths, came Mary Magdalene, and the other Mary, to see the sepulcher."

Mark 16: 1, 2

"And when the Sabbath was past, Mary Magdalene, and Mary, the wife of James, and Salome, bought spices to come and anoint him. And very early in the morning of the first day of the Sabbaths, They come to the tomb at the rising of the sun."

Luke 24:1

"And on the first day of the Sabbaths, very early in the morning, they came to the tomb, carrying the spices which they had prepared, and some women with them."

See Online; http://www.ccel.org/ccel/calvin/calcom33.ii.xlv.html

(Furthermore In Calvin's Logic)...

Acts 20:7

"And upon one day of the Sabbaths, when the disciples were come together to break bread, Paul disputed with them, being about to take his journey on the morrow; and he prolonged his speech until midnight."

"And in one day. Either doth he mean the first day of the week, which was next after the Sabbath, or else some certain Sabbath. Which latter thing may seem to me more probable; for this cause, because that day was more fit for all assembly, according to custom."

(All Quotes End by Jean Calvin 1509 – 1564)

 See Online;

http://www.ccel.org/ccel/calvin/calcom37.viii.ii.html

***

Matthew 5:17 "Think not that I am come to destroy the law, or the prophets: I am not come to destroy, but to fulfil."

Matthew 5:18 "For verily I say unto you, Till heaven and earth pass, one (μια) jot or one (μια) tittle shall in no wise pass from the law, till all be fulfilled."

Matthew 5:19 "Whosoever therefore shall break one (μια) of these least commandments, and shall teach men so, he shall be called the least in the kingdom of heaven: but whosoever shall do and teach them, the same shall be called great in the kingdom of heaven."

***

The Apostles Kept The Sabbath Day!

Acts 13:14 "But when they departed from Perga, they came to Antioch in Pisidia, and went into the synagogue on the sabbath day, and sat down."

Acts 13:27 "For they that dwell at Jerusalem, and their rulers, because they knew Him not, nor yet the voices of the prophets which are read every sabbath day, they have fulfilled them in condemning Him."

Acts 13:42 "And when the Jews were gone out of the synagogue, the Gentiles besought that these words might be preached to them the next sabbath."

Acts 13:44 "And the next sabbath day came almost the whole city together to hear the word of God."

Acts 15:21 "For Moses of old time hath in every city them that preach him, being read in the synagogues every sabbath day."

Acts 16:13 "And on the sabbath we went out of the city by a river side, where prayer was wont to be made; and we sat down, and spake unto the women which resorted thither."

Acts 17:2 "And Paul, as his manner was, went in unto them, and three sabbath days reasoned with them out of the scriptures."

Acts 18:4 "And he reasoned in the synagogue every sabbath, and persuaded the Jews and the Greeks."

***

Colossians 2:16 "Let no man therefore judge you in meat, or in drink, or in respect of an holyday, or of the new moon, or of the sabbath (σαββατων) days:"

Colossians 2:17 "Which are a shadow of things to come; but the body is of Christ."

* Note here that Gentile Christians commonly interpret these passages as a means of justifying Sunday Church worship as indifferent to the observation of God's Sabbath.

Aside from the replacement of the former ordinances shadowing the feast Sabbaths, those days and the Lord's seventh day Sabbath was never abrogated in any regard by the Jewish Apostles. The Apostles under our Lord's direction transformed a new meaning with the Lord's Eucharist.

Acts 12:3 "And because he saw it pleased the Jews, he proceeded further to take Peter also. (Then were the days of unleavened bread.)"

Acts 13:42 "And when the Jews were gone out of the synagogue, the Gentiles besought that these words might be preached to them the next sabbath."

Acts 18:4 "And he reasoned in the synagogue every sabbath, and persuaded the Jews and the Greeks."

Acts 18:21 "But bade them farewell, saying, I must by all means keep this feast that cometh in Jerusalem: but I will return again unto you, if God will. And he sailed from Ephesus."

Acts 20:16 "For Paul had determined to sail by Ephesus, because he would not spend the time in Asia: for he hasted, if it were possible for him, to be at Jerusalem the day of Pentecost."

1 Corinthians 5:8 "Therefore let us keep the feast, not with old leaven, neither with the leaven of malice and wickedness; but with the unleavened bread of sincerity and truth."

1 Corinthians 10:27 "If any of them that believe not bid you to a feast, and ye be disposed to go; whatsoever is set before you, eat, asking no question for conscience sake."

1 Corinthians 16:8 "But I will tarry at Ephesus until Pentecost."

Revelation 1:10 "I was in the Spirit on the Lord's day, and heard behind me a great voice, as of a trumpet,"

Revelation 22:17 "And the Spirit and the bride say, Come. And let him that heareth say, Come. And let him that is at thirst come. And whosoever will, let him take the water of life freely."

Revelation 22:18 "For I testify unto every man that heareth the words of the prophecy of this book, If any man shall add unto these things, God shall add unto him the plagues that are written in this book:"

Revelation 22:19 "And if any man shall take away from the words of the book of this prophecy, God shall take away his part out of the book of life, and out of the holy city, and from the things which are written in this book."

Revelation 22:20 "He which testifieth these things saith, Surely I come quickly. Amen. Even so, come, (Yehoshua) Lord Jesus."

Revelation 22:21 "The grace of our Lord Jesus

(Yehoshua) Christ be with you all. Amen."

* Here we have a loathsome demonstration from a first century writing. (Quotes Begin)

"To kill the rumors, Nero (AD 54-68) charged and tortured some people hated for their evil practices—the group popularly known as 'Christians'. The founder of this sect, Christ, had been put to death by the governor of Judea, Pontius Pilate, when Tiberius was Emperor."

"First those who confessed to being Christians were arrested. Then, on information obtained from them, hundreds were, convicted, more for their anti-social beliefs than for fire-raising. In their deaths they were made a mockery. They were covered in the skins of wild animals, torn to death by dogs, crucified or set on fire so that when darkness fell they burned like torches in the night."

"Nero opened up his own gardens for this spectacle and gave a show in the arena, where he mixed with the crowd, or stood dressed as a charioteer on a chariot. As a result, although they were guilty of being Christians and deserved death, people began to feel sorry for them. For they realized that they were being massacred not for the public good but to satisfy one man's mania." (Quotes End)

Tacitus, Annals 15.44 (~AD 100)

* Furthermore Professor Bruce M. Metzger makes an observation...(Quotes Begin)

"The difference between East and West in the observance of the Sabbath can be accounted for by a reasonable historical explanation. In the West, particularly after the Jewish rebellion under Hadrian, it became vitally important for those who were not Jews to avoid exposing themselves to suspicion; and the observance of the Sabbath was one of the most noticeable indications of Judaism. In the East, however, less opposition was shown to Jewish institutions." (Quotes End)

STUDIES IN LECTIONARY TEXT OF THE GREEK NEW TESTAMENT

By BRUCE M. METZGER, CHICAGO UNIVERSITY PRESS, 1944 > VOL. II, SEC. III, Pg. 12

***

After all things considered we have a statement by the late Dr. Samuele Bacchiocchi. (Quotes Begin)

"The fact that after the year 135 Gentile bishops replaced the bishops of the circumcision...Taking into account the existing restrictions [by Hadrian] which prohibited every form of Jewish worship...it would seem logical to assume that the Gentile Christians adopted Sunday at this time as their day of worship to avoid any possible suspicion of connection with Judaism in the eyes of the Romans." (Quotes End)

ANTI-JUDAISM AND THE ORIGIN OF SUNDAY by SAMUELE BACCHIOCCHI > Pg. 43

THE PONTIFICAL GREGORIAN UNIVERSITY PRESS, ROME, 1975, IMPRIMI POTEST

***

Furthermore he concludes with the origin of Sunday worship as follows. (Quote Begins)

"Epiphanius (ca. AD. 315 – 403) suggests that until A.D. 135 Christians everywhere observed Passover on the Jewish date, namely, on Nisan 15, irrespective of the day of the week... would mean that prior to that time, no necessity had been felt to institute a Sunday memorial (whether annual or weekly) to honor the resurrection."

(Quotes End)

FROM SABBATH TO SUNDAY

by SAMUELE BACCHIOCCHI > Pg. 81

THE PONTIFICAL GREGORIAN UNIVERSITY PRESS, ROME 1977
IMPRIMATUR

The statements above are made in reference to Epiphanius, Adversus haereses 70, 10.

***

* Eusebius had full possession of the earlier writings. He could have forged parts of them to easily suit Constantine's agenda. (Quote Begins)

"We shall introduce into this history in general only those events which may be useful first to ourselves and afterwards to posterity."

(Quote Ends) Eusebius, Ecclesiastical History, Vol. 8, chapter 2. From the Nicene and Post-Nicene Fathers of the Christian Church

Volume 1 Philip Schaff; WM. B. Eerdmans Publishing Company, Grand Rapids, 1956

* Google the image results of Constantine the Great depicting himself equal to a sun god on a Roman coin to understand the depth and conviction of his self infatuation.

The Anti-Judaism Of New Christianity? Constantine speaks at the Council of Nicaea; (Quote Begins)

"Let us have nothing in common with the detestable Jewish crowd; for we have received from our Saviour a different way." (Quote Ends)

'Eusebius': Constantine – The Life of Constantine Chapter Book iii, chapter XVIII

From the Nicene and Post-Nicene Fathers of the Christian Church Volume 1 Philip Schaff; WM. B. Eerdmans Publishing Company, Grand Rapids, 1956

Constantine: The Lord's Day and Day of Preparation Eusebius speaks; (Quotes Begin)

"He ordained, too, that one day should be regarded as a special occasion for prayer: I mean that which is truly the first and chief of all, the day of our Lord and Saviour...Accordingly he enjoined all the subjects of the Roman empire to observe the Lord's day, as a day of rest, and also to honor the day which precedes the Sabbath; in memory, I suppose, of what the Saviour of mankind is recorded to have achieved on that day. And since his desire was to teach his whole army zealously to honor the Saviour's day which derives its name from light and from the sun."

(Quotes End) Eusebius, The Life of Constantine, Book iv, Chapter xviii, From the Nicene and Post – Nicene Fathers of the Christian Church Volume 1 Philip Schaff; WM. B. Eerdmans Publishing Company, Grand Rapids, 1956

***

Constantine Declares Himself an External Bishop to the Church

Eusebius speaks; (Quotes Begin)

"Hence it was not without reason that once, on the occasion of entertaining a company of bishops, he let fall the expression, "that he himself too was a bishop," addressing them in my hearing in the following words:"

"You are bishops whose jurisdiction is within the Church: I also am a bishop, ordained by God to overlook whatever is external to the church." (Quotes End)

– Eusebius, The Life of Constantine, Book iv, Chapter xxiv, From the Nicene and Post-Nicene Fathers of the Christian Church Volume 1 Philip Schaff; WM. B. Eerdmans Publishing Company, Grand Rapids, 1956

See also;

http://www.fordham.edu/halsall/basis/vita-constantine.asp

***

Constantine the Great a Murderer

§7.Chapter One – Fifth Five Years. Eusebius speaks here. (Quotes Begin)

"The beginning of this period was the beginning of the series of acts which have taken most from the reputation of Constantine. Sometime in 326, perhaps while at Rome, he ordered the death of his son Crispus. [3034] The same year (Hieron. Chron.) the Cæsar Licinius, his sister's son, was put to death (Eutrop. 10. 6; Hieron.; Prosper.), and shortly after [3035] his wife Fausta died or was put to death. [3036] But apart from this shadow, the period was hardly less brilliant, in its way, than preceding ones."

(Quotes End) The Prolegomena – Constantine The Great , From the Nicene and Post-Nicene Fathers of the Christian Church Volume 1 Philip Schaff; WM. B. Eerdmans Publishing Company, Grand Rapids, 1956

See Also;

http://mb-soft.com/believe/txub/eusebiuf.html

* Note – All the above events occurred after AD 325 being the Council of Nicaea. Remember Dear Christians, that this Emperor had everything and everyone under his control.

***

Constantine Delays His Christening Until Deathbed Eusebius writes what Constantine speaks; (Quotes Begin)

" The time is arrived which I have long hoped for, with an earnest desire and prayer that I might obtain the salvation of God...After he had thus spoken, the prelates performed the sacred ceremonies...All these events...on the last day of all, which one might call the feast of feasts [Pentecost? Sunday May 22 AD 337], he was removed about midday."

(Quotes End)

Eusebius, The Life of Constantine, Book iv, Chapters LXII – LXIV, From the Nicene and Post-Nicene Fathers of the Christian Church Volume 1 Philip Schaff; WM. B.Eerdmans Publishing Company, Grand Rapids, 1956 See also;

http://www.fordham.edu/halsall/basis/vita-constantine.asp

***

* Again we have a statement from Bruce M. Metzger. (Quotes Begin)

"The transfer of Easter to the first day of the week was no doubt because Sunday had become the Christian weekly day for worship. That this was owing to the Lord's resurrection on Sunday is not provable but suggested strongly by the New Testament evidence and the absence of any convincing alternative theory."

(Quotes End)

THE OXFORD COMPANION TO THE BIBLE > Pg. 173 EDITED BY BRUCE M. METZGER

& MICHAEL D COOGAN

OXFORD UNIVERSITY PRESS 1993

* The late Bruce M. Metzger was a Professor of the Greek New Testament at the Princeton Theological Seminary.

Here we have a statement from a trio of modern day book authors. (Quotes Begin)

"Christianity had hitherto held Saturday, the Jewish Sabbath as sacred. Now in accordance with Constantine's edict, it transferred its sacred day to Sunday."

"The cult of Sol Invictus also meshed happily with that of Mithras... Both emphasized the status of the sun... Both celebrated a major birth festival on December 25th."

Quoted from Pg. 387 of;

THE HOLY BLOOD AND THE HOLY GRAIL by Michael

Baigent, Richard Leigh & Henry Lincoln 1982 ISBN 0-552- 12138-X

***

Socrates speaks 439 BC (Quote Begins)

"Almost all the Churches throughout the world celebrate the sacred mysteries on the sabbath of every week, yet the Christians of Alexandria and at Rome, on account of some ancient tradition, have ceased to do this." (Quote Ends)

Socrates Scholasticus, Ecclesiastical History, Book 5, ch. 22. Translators; Edward Walford, Henri de Valois, Published by; Henry G. Bohn, LONDON: York Street Covent Garden 1853

* This shows that Sunday worship in some parts of the world was well in to affect long before Christianity came.

***

Genesis 2:3 "And God blessed the seventh day, and sanctified it: because that in it he had rested from all his work which God created and made."

Exodus 20:8 "Remember the sabbath day, to keep it holy."

Exodus 20:10 "But the seventh day is the sabbath of the (Civil week) LORD thy God: in it thou shalt not do any work, thou, nor thy son, nor thy daughter, thy manservant, nor thy maidservant, nor thy cattle, nor thy stranger that is within thy gates:"

Exodus 20:11 "For in six days the LORD made heaven and earth, the sea, and all that in them is, and rested the seventh day: wherefore the LORD blessed the sabbath day, and hallowed it."

Exodus 35:2 "Six days shall work be done, but on the seventh day there shall be to you an holy day, a sabbath of rest to the LORD: whosoever doeth work therein shall be put to death."

Leviticus 23:3 "Six days shall work be done: but the seventh day is the sabbath of rest, an holy convocation; ye shall do no work therein: it is the sabbath of the LORD in all your dwellings."

Deuteronomy 5:14 "But the seventh day is the sabbath of the LORD thy God: in it thou shalt not do any work, thou, nor thy son, nor thy daughter, nor thy manservant, nor thy maidservant, nor thine ox, nor thine ass, nor any of thy cattle, nor thy stranger that is within thy gates; that thy manservant and thy maidservant may rest as well as thou."

Matthew 12:6 "But I say unto you, That in this place is one greater than the temple."

Mark 14:58 "We heard Him say, I will destroy this temple that is made with hands, and within three days I will build another made without hands."

Matthew 27:40 "And saying, Thou that destroyest the temple, and buildest it in three days, save thyself. If thou be the Son of God, come down from the cross."

John 2:19 "Jesus answered and said unto them, Destroy this temple, and in three days I will raise it up."

John 2:20 "Then said the Jews, Forty and six years was this temple in building, and wilt thou rear it up in three days?"

John 2:21 "But he spoke, of the temple of His body."

1 Corinthians 6:19. "What, Know ye not that your body is the temple of the Holy Ghost which is in you, which ye have of God, and ye are not your own?"

Revelation 11:19 "And the temple of God was opened in heaven, and there was seen in his temple the ark of his testament: and there were lightning, and voices, and thundering, and an earthquake, and great hail."

Revelation 21:22 "And I saw no temple therein: for the Lord God Almighty and the Lamb are the temple of it."

Hebrews 4:4, 5

For He spake in a certain place of the seventh day on this wise, And God did rest the seventh day from all his works. And in this place again, If they shall enter my rest.

Isaiah 66:23

And it shall come to pass, that from one new moon to another, and from one sabbath to another, shall all flesh come to worship before me, saith the Lord.

The End - May God Bless!

.

The 3 & 3 Factor | AD 34 MTH 12:39,40 ACTS 1:5

3 & 3 FACTOR DAYS	HIGH SABBATHS	WEEKLY SABBATHS

6. Fri Nisan 8

⑧ Sat Nisan 23 3. [1]

㉓ Sun Iyyar 8 [16]

㊳ Mon Iyyar 23 [31]

5. Sat Nisan 9

⑨ Sun Nisan 24 [2]

㉔ Mon Iyyar 9 [17]

㊴ Tue Iyyar 24 [32]

4. Sun Nisan 10

⑩ Mon Nisan 25 [3]

㉕ Tue Iyyar 10 [18]

㊵ Wed Iyyar 25 [33]

3. Mon Nisan 11

⑪ Tue Nisan 26 [4]

㉖ Wed Iyyar 11 [19]

㊶ Thur Iyyar 26 [34]

2. Tue Nisan 12

⑫ Wed Nisan 27 [5]

㉗ Thur Iyyar 12 [20]

㊷ Fri Iyyar 27 [35]

1. Wed Nisan13

⑬ Thur Nisan 28 [6]

㉘ Fri Iyyar 13 [21]

㊸ Sat Iyyar 28 [36]

Pass. Thur Nisan 14

⑭ Fri Nisan 29 [7]

㉙ Sat Iyyar 14 [22]

㊹ Sun Iyyar 29 [37]

Fri Nisan 15

⑮ Sat Nisan 30 [8]

㉚ Sun Iyyar 15 [23]

㊺ Mon Sivan 1 [38]

① Sat Nisan 16

⑯ Sun Iyyar 1 [9]

㉛ Mon Iyyar 16 [24]

㊻ Tue Sivan 2 [39]

② Sun Nisan 17

⑰ Mon Iyyar 2 [10]

㉜ Tue Iyyar 17 [25]

㊼ Wed Sivan 3 ^[40]

③ Mon Nisan 18

⑱ Tue Iyyar 3 [11]

㉝ Wed Iyyar 18 [26]

㊽ Thur Sivan 4 1.

④ Tue Nisan 19

⑲ Wed Iyyar 4 [12]

㉞ Thur Iyyar 19 [27]

㊾ Fri Sivan 5 2.

⑤ Wed Nisan 20 ✝

⑳ Thur Iyyar 5 [13]

㉟ Fri Iyyar 20 [28]

㊿ Sat Sivan 6 3.

⑥ Thur Nisan 21 1.

㉑ Fri Iyyar 6 [14]

㊱ Sat Iyyar 21 [29]

Passover Feast:
Pentecost Count: ① - ㊿
Crucifixion Day: ✝
Resurrected Days: [1] - [40]
Ascension Day: ^

⑦ Fri Nisan 22 2.

㉒ Sat Iyyar 7 [15]

㊲ Sun Iyyar 22 [30]

Printed in Great Britain
by Amazon

59479120R00119